Noel Turnbull is one of Australia's leading PR strategists and corporate communications specialists, an expert in community attitudes and corporate responses. He is the founding chairman of Turnbull Fox Phillips, the largest Australian-owned public relations firm and a member of the Worldcom Group internationally. His campaigns for a range of private companies and public bodies have won awards from the International Association of Business Communicators, the International Public Relations Association and the Public Relations Institute of Australia, of which he is a Fellow.

Educated at the University of Melbourne, and having served as an artillery officer in Vietnam, Noel worked in journalism and as a parliamentary press secretary before entering public relations. His eclectic involvement in the community has seen him write *A History of Port Melbourne* (OUP, 1983), act as a Councillor for that city, serve as Chair of the National Book Council and on the board of the *Australian Book Review.* Currently, he is Chair of Visions of Australia, the Australian Government's exhibition touring grants committee, and of the RMIT Communications Faculty Advisory Committee.

THE MILLENNIUM EDGE

Prospering with Generation MM

Noel Turnbull

ALLEN & UNWIN

First published in 1996 by
Allen & Unwin Pty Ltd
9 Atchison Street, St Leonards, NSW 2065 Australia
Phone: (61 2) 9901 4088
Fax: (61 2) 9906 2218
E-mail: frontdesk@allen-unwin.com.au
URL: http://www.allen-unwin.com.au

National Library of Australia
Cataloguing-in-Publication entry:

Turnbull, Noel 1946– .
The millennium edge: prospering with generation MM.

Includes index.
ISBN 1 86448 237 0.

1. Twenty-first century—Forecasts. I. Title.

303.40905

Set in 10.5/12 pt Baskerville by DOCUPRO, Sydney
Printed by Australian Print Group, Maryborough, Victoria

10 9 8 7 6 5 4 3 2 1

Contents

Preface

On the stroke of midnight on Friday 31 December 1999† one millennium will end and another will begin.

From a strictly rational viewpoint it will be just another New Year's Eve. Yet already the British Government has established a Millennium Commission to plan for the years after it. Thousands of religious groups are preparing for the end of the world. The exclusive Rainbow Room in New York is booked out for the night. Political and environmental groups are anticipating the apocalypse, and the Pope is warning Rome's local government authorities that more than 30 million worshippers will descend on the Vatican, creating traffic and accommodation havoc.

So, while to some the year 2000 may be just another year, millions of others believe that the millennium is something more. And because they believe it is different—beyond the normal—they will behave differently and by doing so make it different.

Following the turn of the last millennium—a thousand years ago—there were centuries of massive social and religious upheaval. People believed the world was ending and, in preparation, put on sackcloth, covered themselves in ashes, whipped themselves with flails and looked to changes in the weather and to unusual or inexplicable events as portents of the apocalypse. Historians have called this movement 'millenarianism'.

Today, the millennium's approach is encouraging the growth of new forms of millenarianism. Combined with the revolutionary social, economic and technological changes the world is experiencing, this new millenarian thinking is compounding the massive uncertainties of business, politics and life. It is changing how we organise companies and motivate staff; it is changing how we market our products and how we communicate with each other; it is changing national and global political structures and priorities; and it is changing our vision of what is valuable to us as individuals—with all the lifestyle implications that such a change creates.

But despite the uncertainty and the irrationality, it is possible to understand the motivations behind this mystical interest in the millennium. And when we understand it, when we demystify it, we will be better able to anticipate change, plan for it and gain a millennium edge.

† The debate on the true date for the new millennium will rage across the letters pages of quality broadsheets in the next few years. The true, mathematical and rational eve of the millennium may well be 31 December 2000. But the *psychologically revelent* eve will certainly be a year earlier, as we wait for the 2 to clock over on the calendars everywhere. And, as we shall see, such perceptions create their own reality.

Acknowledgements

The author wishes to acknowledge the invaluable research assistance provided by Kylie Oakes and Therase Keating. Rosemary Sorensen provided the initial impetus for the book and made perceptive editorial suggestions. Lisa Interligi suggested the Generation MM concept. Annie Delbridge processed the manuscript through its various permutations. Joshua Dowse was an encouraging and insightful publisher.

Welcome to the millennium

At a recent conference in Paris—the birthplace of modern rational views of the world—I was chatting to a very charming American businessman. He was drinking water and I was drinking wine. But apart from that we seemed to be agreeing on things: trends in communication and technology and great places to visit in the city.

Suddenly, impelled by something I can't recall, he said: 'But Jesus Christ will tell me what to do'. Being a typical baby-boomer rationalist, as embarrassed by religious fervour as by old-fashioned social symbols, I ignored the comment and soon escaped before I heard more than I wanted to about salvation and similar things. The episode reminded me that many Americans today live the life described by Catherine Blake when she said of her husband, the famous poet, William: 'I have very little of Mr Blake's company; he is always in Paradise'.

A few days later, *The Economist* ran an article about environmentalists and religious leaders getting together to discuss common beliefs in the apocalypse and how it might be averted. This immediately brought to mind the mass of market research and social data on the re-emergence of religion in modern society. In the United States creationists are battling to have creation science taught alongside evolution in schools. Huge percentages of Americans consistently report that they believe in God, Satan, resurrection, the apocalypse and the imminent end of the world.

Significantly, the article—which I discuss in more detail in Chapter 3—linked the apocalypse with the environment.

All this put into a new context the work I had been doing for almost a decade in helping companies and other organisations to cope with the immense changes they were confronting. It also made me realise there were growing signs that the millenarian thinking that has surfaced among humans at various intervals in history was again emerging—in the final years before the new millennium.

Later I will describe what millenarian thinking involves and something of its history. But first we need to look at the signs of its advent. The fundamental sign is an apocalyptic belief—a belief in the end of the world as it has been known. Indications of this belief emerged for me in the context of my environmental work.

Over the years I had spent many weeks working with forestry, chemical, manufacturing and property companies, helping them explain their policies and performance to communities and to activists. At first the task was straightforward—to convince companies that the solution to environmental problems was not better communication but real changes in performance; and to show communities what real changes were occurring.

But as the years went by the task changed. It became a matter of trying to encourage dialogue between groups who were eons apart in approach and attitude. Radical environmentalists were convinced that the end of the world was imminent and that the impending apocalypse justified direct action. Company managers were convinced that the activists were incapable of understanding simple technical and economic arguments. The general public, watching the conflict, was confused, uncertain and frightened, but seemed prepared to believe the environmentalists' warning that the globe faced disaster. The vision becoming common was of a world destroyed by the drive for profit—of mutant creatures and dead rivers and oceans denuded of birds and fish.

During this period I wrote speeches, pamphlets, mission statements, employee briefing notes and submissions to government inquiries, talking about the unprecedented upheavals occurring in the competitive position of companies and the need for continuous change to cope with it. I found that most managers, public servants, journalists and politicians agreed on the basic message and on what needed to be done.

But while *they* agreed on the need for change, the majority of the population saw a different future—more chaotic and uncertain. Their vision was not of a vibrant, rational and competitive world. Their vision was driven by anxiety and uncertainty and by a dread that the world as they had known it was ending. Like some environmentalists they had developed a vision of apocalypse now.

In order to survive and prosper in the 21st century, business needs to understand how this apocalyptic vision has been formed, what it involves, how to respond to it and even how it might, without business people realising it, be shaping some of their own decisions. This is a doubly important challenge for business because business itself is being buffeted by the same change and uncertainty that is driving millenarian beliefs.

Businesses' careful marketing plans—along with governments' economic policies—are undermined by seemingly irrational and unanticipated consequences of new technological developments and other phenomena. In the United States the huge oil company Exxon faces boycotts from fundamentalist Christians because its company logo is believed to be a symbol of Satan. Intel, the giant microchip manufacturer, faced a crisis when subterranean criticism of its latest product spread rapidly across the Internet—unseen by many marketing managers or the business media. There are many such examples.

Day in and day out, governments and companies make predictions and form plans concerning the marketplace and the economy. Day in and day out, their predictions and plans might be derailed by the consequences of (often remote) chaotic phenomena. You may have heard the chaos theory story of the butterfly flapping its wings on one side of the world and causing a tornado on the other side. That analogy captures the point nicely.

APOCALYPSE NOW

The apocalyptic vision isn't formed just by the sweeping changes facing society. It is also formed by the accretion of day-to-day incidents, by new perceptions of information and by the daily fare provided by the news media.

A technical manager in a government instrumentality which had been reorganised, and its staff slashed, once used biblical language in talking to me of the change. 'I have been punished', he said. I thought at first he meant that he had been reprimanded or that some other disciplinary action had been taken against him. Instead, he saw himself as being condemned to a living purgatory—left in an organisation denuded of his friends, forced to work long and exhausting hours and constantly battered by change which had long ceased to have any apparent reason.

Driving across the border between Eire and Northern Ireland recently, I was surprised to see that there was not one guard or staffed checkpoint. Only the change on road signs from miles to kilometres revealed that we had moved from one country to another. Two days later, the entire border had been slammed shut by thousands of police and soldiers. The cause: not the re-emergence of terrorism, but the threat of mad cow disease and a determination to keep British cattle out of the Irish Republic. In strictly commercial terms it was probably a sensible decision. But the contrast in response was a vivid reminder of how people react to risk and to apocalyptic fears.

Some colleagues I had planned to meet in Northern Ireland were reluctant to come. The end of the ceasefire made it too dangerous, a Californian said—despite the fact that the total number of children shot and killed *in Los Angeles schools in any one year* is more than all the lives lost in Britain and Ireland to murders and terrorism in any one year.

The World Health Organisation claims that TB will kill 30 million people in the next decade. In 1900 it killed 2.1 million people. Today—because of population increases, the failure of control programs and the rise of HIV—it is killing 3 million people a year. That's 10 000 times as many people killed each year as fall victim to the Ebola virus. In the United Kingdom, there are 6000 new TB patients a year and 400 deaths. BSE ('mad cow disease'), in contrast, has so far caused ten confirmed deaths.

In all these cases the responses were driven by a sense of unimagined, and often unimaginable, threats. The technical manager should, according to top management, have been delighted and motivated by having been selected as a valuable and continuing part of the team. That—rationally—was what had happened. His perception, however, was of punishment and purgatory. The exotic health risks, however statistically improbable, were perceived as being more real and immediate threats to personal safety and to global humanity than were the mundane.

And daily the world seems to many to be more dangerous and unstable than at any time since World War II. The Cold War's end was supposed to usher in a new world order, but parts of Russia are a battleground again. In Africa, society after society is disintegrating into endless civil war, famine and economic chaos. Some adherents of Islam are threatening a holy war—a jihad—against the West. A state, Iran, has declared a fatwa on a writer, Salman Rushdie, who is alleged to have committed blasphemy in one of his books. Communal violence continues in India, Africa, Bosnia and the Russian near east. A peasant revolutionary army, equipped with fax and Internet addresses, has emerged in Mexico. Holy war continues in Afghanistan. Some inner urban United States cities look like World War II bombsites inhabited by the violent and the drug-addicted.

New plagues—AIDS and the Ebola virus—are around the world. There are also warnings that a potentially deadly flu pandemic, worse than that of 1918, is about to appear.

Global media daily spell out the dimensions of these disasters and herald each new event as more frightening than the last. The Four Horsemen of the Apocalypse appear to be riding into the living spaces of the world through people's television screens and the pages of their newspapers.

THE COUNTDOWN BEGINS

This apocalyptic vision is emerging as we count down to an event of immense psychological significance—the end of the millennium. A few years ago the word was hardly heard outside religious and sociological circles. Yet, as each day before the turn of the century goes by, someone else starts to focus attention on the idea.

The first history of the millennium in which we live has now been published; symptomatic of the new globalism, it is written in English by an academic of Spanish descent, Felipe Fernandez Armesto. The University of California Press is publishing a series of volumes called *Poems for the Millennium.* The United Kingdom Government has established its Millennium Commission, which is giving away one billion pounds raised from the national lottery for projects that benefit the community and, most importantly, provide inspiration for Britain's entry into the new millennium. The Royal Albert Hall in London, like the Rainbow Room on top of New York's Radio City, was booked for New Year's Eve 1999 twenty-five years ago. And Felipe Fernandez Armesto tells us that a Millennium Society of London and New York has been created and that it is planning a party at the pyramids in Egypt.

Urban myths about the millennium are also beginning to appear. A typical example is the story that computers cannot cope with date changes after 1999 and that, when midnight strikes, computers around the world will crash. The *New Scientist* reported on 13 January 1996 that a British MP, David Atkinson, had written to the Prime Minister asking if he were aware of the problems that industry faced and asking what was going to be done about it. While it is true that some older computers could crash, most modern equipment does not have a problem—and much of the obsolete equipment will have been phased out by the year 2000. Nevertheless, the British Government has referred the matter to a committee which will report—presumably before midnight—on what can be done.

This growing fascination with the millennium is a heightened form of people's fascination with significant numbers. In fact, the numbers in themselves are not really significant at all. The calendar itself has been changed three times in the past 2000 or so years. In 46 BC Julius Caesar reformed the Roman calendar by adding 90 days to the year to get the northern spring back to its traditional March period. In 10 BC it had to be changed again because leap years had been counted incorrectly. Another inbuilt mistake caused the calendar to get a further ten days out of kilter by 1582—when Pope Gregory XIII reformed it again and tidied up the counting of leap years.

The French adopted the new Gregorian system in 1582 and the English in 1750. The Russians didn't adopt the new calendar until 1918, magically making the Bolshevik November revolution the October revolution that it has been to historians ever since!

Around the world New Year's Day occurs on different dates in different societies. It may be 1 January in the Gregorian calendar, but the Chinese New Year for 1996 was 19 February. The Burmese date was 15 April, the Islamic 19 May, the Zoroastrian 28 July and the Jewish 14 September. In all, about fifteen significant 'New Year's Days' can be identified in any given year.

The European millennium happens to coincide with the beginning of a period the Japanese call *seiki-matsu*—the end of a century and also a millennium—which is expected to bring uncertainty and a state of flux.

And strictly speaking—although noone but pedants will pursue the point—the millennium doesn't really start until 1 January 2001.

However, it is not the objective reality that matters. Calendars may change and different societies may mark different days as the beginning of their new year. But the people in the currently dominant global society, the West, believe that the date 2000 is significant and—because they believe it is significant—it is significant.

MILLENARIAN THINKING, WHERE DID IT COME FROM?

The two developments—apocalyptic vision and the looming advent of the millennium itself—have created fertile ground for the emergence of millenarian thinking. But millenarian thinking comes in many guises, and has a long history.

Four millennia ago most societies had a static view of the world. It existed and it went on—just as life went on. The first historian of millenarianism, Norman Cohn, suggests that the first person to challenge the static view of the world and predict the emergence of a new perfect world was the Iranian prophet Zarathustra—commonly known as Zoroaster—although the name is more commonly associated, in the 19th and 20th centuries, with a book by Nietzsche and a very successful rock band! At some time between 1400 and 1500 BC, Cohn says, Zoroaster developed a new religion which still survives, although with less than a million adherents.The religion appears to have been inspired by tensions in Iranian society between two ways of life—peaceful pastoralists and ruthless bands of warriors. Zoroaster's work, the *Gathas*, reflected the tensions and miseries of this conflict and predicted a great transformation by a process described by words meaning the 'making wonderful'. The 'making wonderful' was to change everything, eliminate imperfection and create a changeless world in which everyone would live in peace and prosperity forever. Before we scoff at the relevance of a religious prophet from three and half thousand years ago, it is well to listen to the echoes of 'making wonderful' in much modern marketing and political campaigning.

In an essay in *Apocalypse Theory and the Ends of the World*[1] Norman Cohn asks:

> What, one wonders, could have led a man living around 1400 BC, in a predominantly pastoral society somewhere in Central Asia, to decide that the troubled world he knew would shortly be utterly changed, transformed into a perfect world? In ancient societies the world, though essentially unchanging, was nevertheless felt to be constantly threatened by chaotic forces. In many societies this feeling was given expression in myths of the kind known to scholars as combat myths. Combat myths tell how, when the ordered world is about to be engulfed by chaos and catastrophe, a hero steps forward, defeats the chaos and saves the world.

Before we dismiss such beliefs as primitive superstitions we need to reflect that combat myths are still the basic ingredient of the comics, novels and films that form the staple entertainment diet of many of today's young people and adults. They have also underpinned much of the international and domestic political debates and divisions of the 20th century. The beliefs may be superstitious but so—still—is the world in which we live.

Some historians say that the Zoroastrian myth influenced the millenarian ideas that did most to shape Western millenarian thinking—the ideas stemming from Christian doctrine concerning 'the last times' or the 'last days' based on the Book of Revelation in the Bible. The Book of Revelation was probably composed towards the end of the reign of the Roman Emperor Domitian—around 95–96 AD. It was interpreted by early Christians as predicting the Second Coming of Christ, who would establish a kingdom on earth over which he would reign for 1000 years before the Last Judgement. In recent decades, however, the term millenarianism, which derives originally from that Christian doctrine, has been interpreted much more widely and has become a label for any type of salvation belief. In the book which launched a thousand studies on the subject, *The Pursuit of the Millennium*,[2] Cohn suggests that a series of common characteristics are exhibited by millenarian sects and movements. Such movements see salvation as:

- collective—to be enjoyed by all the faithful who believe in the vision
- terrestrial—to be enjoyed on earth and not in some other-worldly heaven
- imminent—it will come soon and suddenly
- total—it will utterly transform life on earth so that the new system will not just be an improvement on the present but perfection
- miraculous—in the sense that it will be helped by supernatural agencies.

Not all millenarian sects are exactly the same, but many of today's radical religious, political or environmental movements show that the characteristics Cohn describes are useful tools to help us understand otherwise strange phenomena.

The imminent and miraculous nature of the salvation is generally linked to an apocalyptic view of the world in which, Cohn says, the world is dominated by an evil, tyrannous power of boundless destructiveness—a power which is imagined not as simply human but as demonic. The tyranny of that power will become more and more outrageous, the sufferings of its victims more and more intolerable, until suddenly the hour will strike when the 'chosen' are able to rise up and overthrow it.

This apocalyptic tradition is epitomised by the vision in the Book of Daniel in the Bible in which four beasts 'shall devour the whole earth, and shall tread it down, and break it in pieces'. In later prophecies this became the Four Horsemen of the Apocalypse—hunger, war, civil strife and death.

Numbers are very important in millenarianism. There is a tradition in millenarian predictions, based on three phases: the signs of the apocalypse; the spreading of the faith; and the triumph in which the faithful are rewarded for a thousand years. It is often argued that Hitler's Third Reich—claimed to be set to last for 1000 years—is part of this tradition.

These traditional fantasies about apocalypses influenced the way in which people viewed political and economic developments, but it was only in certain social circumstances that they took hold and became a dominant factor in shaping behaviour and belief.

Ironically, the year 1000 is not the best example of such times, although it was the subject of some millenarian hopes and beliefs. There was, according to the historian Krishan Kumar in *Apocalypse Theory and the Ends of the World,*[3] 'considerable tension and terror in the middle of the tenth century and at somewhat earlier and later times—though not, it appears, in the year 1000 itself'.

What is clear is that various Christians believed that the year 1000 would be significant. St Augustine expected that as the millennium had begun with the birth of Christ then it must end a thousand years later. In Britain the Venerable Bede announced that the end of the world would come in the year 1000 and many other Christian thinkers endorsed his views.

Krishan Kumar, in describing these developments, identifies another phenomenon of great importance to us today: 'In one of those repeated examples of the consequences of the failure of prophecy, expectations of the end of the world intensified and multiplied after the year 1000'. In other words, the failure of the prophecy did not remove the concern from community thinking but rather intensified it.

After the year 1000, the circumstances which foster millenarian thinking occurred often between the 12th and 16th centuries in Europe. Cohn attributes the circumstances to rapid social changes: in particular the collapse of the manorial system, the advent of the plague which killed one-third of the European population, materialism replacing traditional social links, massive uncertainty created by urbanisation and changes in work, widespread poverty, and natural disasters (circumstances all remarkably similar to some which apply today). A striking example of the resulting public despair was the outbreak of mass self-flagellation which started in Italy in 1258. There had been famine, a serious plague outbreak and incessant civil war, and the country had been reduced to a state of misery and chronic insecurity.

Since Cohn's pioneering work many other scholars have extended and revised his theories. There are now structuralist, Marxist, neo-Marxist, post-modernist and other theories of millenarain thinking.

This later research has shifted the academic emphasis on millenarianism more towards the insights of the great sociologist, Max Weber, who saw it as a response to massive social change, a sense of fear and evil and a desire for salvation. This emphasis on salvation is the best perspective from which to view modern millenarian beliefs.

Millenarian ideas were strongly anti-commercial and often contained beliefs that all wealth would be redistributed—control of assets would be wrenched from churches, landowners, political leaders and so on. Down the centuries we have seen similar sects and movements with similar ideas about the new world. From Cromwell and Marx to Adam Smith and Ronald Reagan, millenarian thinking has driven policy and attitudes.

In the 17th century, during the English civil war, many religious groups believed the Second Coming was nigh. It has been argued that one of the reasons why Oliver Cromwell lifted the restrictions on Jews living in England—brutally implemented by Simon de Montfort four centuries before—was that the conversion of the Jews was said to precede the Second

Coming. A more plausible reason is Cromwell's relative religious tolerance.

In an essay in *Cargo Cults and Millenarian Movements*[4] Dennis Walker points out that the Black Muslim movement has a strongly millenarian strand in its beliefs and believes that 'after the Last Judgement the righteous blacks would inherit authority over the whole globe, bringing the "new Islam" the final age of eternal peace and happiness'. Louis Farrakhan, the African-American political leader who successfully mounted the 1995 Million Man March on Washington, is a millenarian. Walker recounts:

> Even in September 1985, his journal *Final Call* reported that Farrakhan had been 'beamed up on board a space craft' to hear the voice of Elijah Muhammad expose a military plot by President Reagan; and there were claims that God's 'angelic hosts' were working to support Farrakhan 'in conjunction with an Intergalactic Federation of Star Brothers' as the modern Babylon's 'final days' approached. Farrakhan, then, while playing down the Armageddon scenario in his public rhetoric, as well as Elijah's projection of Judgement Day to destroy the whites, has not completely repressed the millenarian impetus in the ranks of the sectlet.

Obviously the claims are ridiculous, but they are being made by a man who managed to encourage one million African-Americans to march on Washington in the biggest such protest since the days of Martin Luther King.

Nor are millenarian beliefs confined to African-Americans. A United States television evangelist and Republican candidate for President, Pat Robertson, is a firm believer in the apocalypse. And the former United States President, Ronald Reagan, is alleged to have told another evangelist, Jim Bakker: 'We may be the generation which sees Armageddon'.[5]

The two dominant ideologies of the 20th century, Marxism and capitalism, reflect millenarian thinking in their most extreme forms. In the case of Marxists, the combat myth—class struggle—will lead to the perfect society. In the case of doctrinaire free enterprise theorists, 'the invisible hand' of perfect competition will ensure the best of all possible worlds. Marx

never defined precisely what a perfect communist s
would be like. Adam Smith, much referred to and rarely
would almost certainly be horrified by the claims made in
name. But both—like Zoroaster in 1400 BC—have inspir
millenarianism.

Millenarian beliefs, apocalyptic or utopian, are not confined to the fringes of society and politics. For almost four millennia they have, at significant points in history, had profound influence. We are at such a point again.

millennium edge

This book is concerned with why business needs to recognise the significance of these millenarian signs and how it can win a competitive edge from understanding what they mean. The fundamental thing we must remember is that, just as 20th century society was different from that of the 19th century, so 21st century society will be different from ours. It will be a new century with new technologies, new values, new approaches to knowledge—and most importantly, a new generation of people.

I can't tell you what to do to prepare for these new developments in the 21st century. I can only tell you what you might need to know. With a wider knowledge of emerging trends, it will be possible to apply your own intelligence and powers of innovation to the key areas of business, politics, technology and economics in order to gain the millennium edge.

What you should know about the new millennium is dictated by four considerations.

First: why the emerging millenarianism is important and how it will influence what people think about 21st century business and society.

Second: why what people think—their perception of things—is crucially important to what they do and how reality is shaped.

Third: what the fundamental social, technological and economic factors shaping the structure of the 21st century world will be.

Fourth: what the first generation of the 21st century—the cohort I call Generation MM—will demand from the world.

These four developments are creating a gap between what managers and companies think and what the general population, their consumers, believe.

The millennium edge comes from developing the foresight and flexibility and the insight and intelligence which enables companies to close the gap.

The millennium edge does not come from some fashionable management tool. Instead it is based on an attitude of mind—a new approach to everything that business does.

That attitude of mind allows managers to understand that the chasm exists. And then it equips them to shape their corporate cultures; create new organisational structures; communicate with consumers in new ways; and develop a genuine empathy for the changes which are transforming communities, political structures and nations.

Business must learn to think like Generation MM or miss out.

That means having values; being a committed and responsible member of the community; communicating through dialogue rather than didactically; and learning that in the millennium perceptions count as much as performance.

The concepts concerning values and responsibility underpin the principles which all outstanding 20th century companies espouse.

The secret to the millennium edge, however, is understanding the way in which the 21st century world is transforming the environment in which business must apply the principles and how Generation MM is giving new meanings to the principles themselves.

When business demonstrates that it does understand, Generation MM will repay that understanding with trust. And in 21st century—as we will see—it is the trusted companies which will succeed.

WHY IS MILLENARIANISM IMPORTANT?

There have always been small groups of people thinking that the world will end or be totally transformed at any moment. Why are they more important today than before?

The major reason is that today they are no longer small groups—they represent significant sections of the population throughout the world. As we have seen, they include African-Americans marching in a million-strong formation on Washington. As we will see shortly, they also include the disparate groups that make up what are known as New Agers. They include both religious fundamentalists and the extreme radical environmentalists. Through the media and modern communications they have access beyond their immediate communities to people around the world. And, most importantly, their messages resonate with those people.

If you have ever visited the Imperial War Museum in London you will begin to understand why. The Museum is in the building once known as the Bethlehem Royal—commonly known as Bedlam. The present building was completed in 1815. It and its predecessors had been used to house the insane, who were chained to walls and presented to the visiting public as a sort of freak show. Visiting the Museum, and knowing its history as Bedlam, shapes your vision of the insanity recorded in its present incarnation as a military museum.

Deep in the Museum is one particularly powerful exhibit—an exhibit which sums up much about the 20th century. It is a simple clockface, with one hand which goes around quite rapidly. Below it is a panel showing numbers. One sweep of the hand represents five people who have died as a result of war during this century. The panel records the total after each sweep—somewhere around 68 million on my last visit. By 31 December 1999 the panel will read 100 000 000—the rough estimate of all of the deaths of all of the wars of this century.

Death, destruction and doom have been an integral part of the 20th century. Two major world wars, dozens of civil wars and other wars. Genocidal policies directed against Jews, the Romany people, Armenians. These are the overwhelmingly important events of our century.

Equally, we have experienced astonishing technological, social and economic change. After one world war an estimated 20 million people around the world died of a massive influenza epidemic; a few years later a massive economic depression swept the world; a few more years and another world war took place. In the second half of the century we reached the Moon in a spacecraft, while similar rocket technology created the ever-present threat of nuclear annihilation.

When the economic boom after the second of the century's world wars gathered pace we discovered that it was happening at the expense of the quality of our waterways and our air. In 100 years we have experienced perhaps thirty years or so in economic boom times and the rest in war, depression, recession or economic change. In recent decades the economic change has been characterised by massive social and technological change, which has disoriented many and fostered anxiety.

It is hardly any wonder that we have created a population of people who see an apocalypse just around the corner and hope that someone can transform their lives by 'making things wonderful', just as Zoroaster promised all those centuries ago. We have created a paradoxical world. One marked by both massive technological achievement and massive destruction. In the context of this 20th century reality we must ask ourselves—why wouldn't millenarian thinking seem attractive to so many?

PERCEPTION IS REALITY

Not only does millenarian thinking seem attractive; it provides a framework of belief which explains to people how an otherwise incomprehensible world works.

In much of the past, what people *did* shaped what they thought. The daily rituals of life in an agricultural field, or the tangible satisfaction of hand-crafting a product, were an ever present reality for the vast majority of people. Today's reality, though, is shaped by bewildering advertising messages, by competing communication channels, by cartoons, film, television and all the masses of popular entertainment that we are confronted with. The young are more likely to have seen Mel Gibson in the film *Braveheart* than to have read anything about the history of Scotland and William Wallace. Even if they had, the film would probably appear more vivid and real than the book. I can never think of any of the Roman emperors without immediately having in mind the faces of the actors who performed in the BBC television serial *I Claudius.*

In such a society myth, fiction, images and reality all get confused to the extent that it is very often difficult to tell which is which. For many people they all merge into one and what they perceive and think becomes their reality. Educators, marketers, businesses and governments need to recognise that this broad trend in people's perceptions is shaping the outlook for the 21st century.

What is clear is that, whether the impetus be millenarianism, the millennium itself or the change and uncertainty, its most important impact will be in the way it shapes what people think about the world. The challenge is to understand that how you communicate with people—how you influence their thinking and help them shape their sense of reality—will be crucial in 21st century success—in gaining the millennium edge.

THE BIG CONFLICT: GLOBALISM VERSUS LOCALISM

We have seen why millenarianism is an important movement and how significant perceptions are in influencing what people think, to the extent even that fiction can appear stronger than fact. We need also to recognise that they are both important in the context of a vital global development that brings together all the diverse social, technological and economic changes of today.

That global development is brought home to me every time I travel overseas and meet business people from different countries and cultures. In Canada or Puerto Rico I will talk to colleagues about changes in telecommunications technology. We will speculate on likely stockmarket movements in our respective nations. We will consult each other about our success in marketing the same products. Most of our conversations will be in a common language—English.

And then, just as we are thinking we are citizens of the one world, some little cultural trait or belief will appear and remind us that we are not as similar as we think. It might be as simple as the frequency with which one eats nachos compared with poached eggs. It might be an attitude to an historical character—a hero to one nation and a villain to another. Or it might be as simple as crossing from the United States into Canada and suddenly noticing that the war memorials now record 1914–1918 and 1939–1945 rather than 1917–1918 and 1941–1945.

What we are seeing at the moment as the most important global development shaping the 21st century is the growing tension between globalism and localism—between supranationalism and separatism. Technology and political change are making the globe smaller and smaller, markets are becoming more global, while at the same time localism is becoming more and more important. This paradox is not surprising. Technology has made it possible for us to transmit words, data and images from almost anywhere in the world to almost anywhere else almost instantly. We can watch sporting contests or the aftermath of disasters while they happen. Financial markets can dislocate economies by shifting trillions of dollars in a nanosecond.

Companies are also becoming genuinely multinational and successful brands are admired around the world. Ford, Coca-Cola, Disney, McDonalds—the brands are almost the world's only universal language. Some years ago I listened to an Australian marketer explaining how Americans simply could not understand the Australian market and how they were inevitably doomed to failure. I couldn't help remarking that this must be why Australians drove Fords, ate at McDonalds, went to Blockbuster Video stores and wore baseball caps back to front!

The business community has come to take much of this globalisation for granted—as much a part of life as switching on a light or picking up a traditional telephone. Its members travel the world knowing that wherever they go they will be welcomed in a Ritz Carlton or a Sheraton which has their preferences on computer. They embrace change and are the leading voices claiming that it is both necessary and inevitable.

Yet while many take it for granted that these trends are

orld more homogeneous, they are actually
e diverse.

e two reasons for this apparent paradox. First, the globalisation of markets makes the case for smaller nations and communities more compelling rather than less. Within a free trade area—where tariffs are abolished and governmental monetary policy is shaped more by international markets than by central banks—the case for stronger and larger nation states is diminished, as economic sovereignty is no longer linked to size.

The Canadian Quebecois separatist intellectual Daniel Latouche talks about people's obsession with the lines they draw to define themselves in the face of this reality. They cannot put up a barrier—a line—against the impact of supranational financial institutions or global change. But they can draw or erect a fence around themselves and their families, their homes, their communities and their nations.

The examples of the tension between supranationalism and separatism are myriad. The United Nations is playing a much larger role in the world at a time when the actual number of independent nations is growing. The European Union is deepening its ties and broadening its membership while individual countries and communities within it are asserting their cultural difference more strongly. One of the fundamental arguments for separatism in Quebec is that sovereignty is made possible by free trade—that the nation can be defined in cultural terms without impacting on the economic outlook. While many Canadians (and half the inhabitants of Quebec) disagree, the separatists' argument is ultimately financially correct.

In simple terms, the more global the world becomes the more possible it is for smaller communities to be both politically and geographically separate while still being part of the wider world.

The second reason for the paradox is a human reason—the human response to change. Change and uncertainty unsettle the vast majority of people. They become frightened and apprehensive. The more change the more fear, and the more fear the more people become alienated and despairing. The greater the despair and the alienation the greater the desire to develop a sense of belonging and security. Thus, as the world becomes more global, the more important it becomes for individuals to define themselves in terms of place, family and community.

From Quebec separatism to the Australian desire to remove the monarch and create a distinctive identity, societies are asserting their distinctiveness at the very time that international markets are treating them all as simply sets of numbers about inflation, exports and budgets on a common global computer screen.

The significance of all of this is that the gap between the business community's acceptance of global financial realities and the individual's search for security can become a gap between companies and their customers and communities. Failure to understand that the gap exists—and the failure to bridge it—will inevitably lead to fundamental strategic mistakes.

GENERATION MM IS BORN

In the midst of all of this a new generation is being born. Society has often sought to characterise decades or generations with tidy phrases. The Roaring Twenties gave birth to the flapper generation, the 1950s to the 'Beat' generation and the 1960s to the hippy generation. The 1980s were said to have created the 'me' generation and the 1990s have been a reaction against the materialist excesses of the eighties.

While the generations may change, and the decades may differ, most of those of us alive today have been shaped by the 20th century and all the extremes associated with it. It has been our century and, whether we like it or not, its events are part of our lives.

We now have, however, an increasing number of people being born who will live the majority of their lives in the 21st century and be shaped by the events of that century, whatever they may be.

Just as many of those living in the 20th century sought to reject the 19th century, so it is inevitable that many in this new generation will seek to reject the 20th century. Others of them—as some 20th century people idealised the 19th century—will idealise our century and project upon it an imagined glorious past. Whether it is rejection or idealisation, they will be reacting to the 20th century rather than being part of it. They will, truly, be a new generation, the first 21st century generation. They will inherit all the consequences of the dramatic change that the world is experiencing, all the apocalyptic fears and the millenarian hopes.

As yet most of them are only dimly glimpsing—if at all—this new reality. But eventually, some time after the year 2000, its logic will become obvious.

Because it is the millennium it is convenient to term this new generation Generation MM, drawing on the Roman numeral for the number 2000.

What will a typical individual from Generation MM be like? What will they think and what will they do?

Most importantly, they will be the inheritors of the benefits of the 20th century. As we have seen, the 20th century generations have lived through the paradox of technological achievement side by side with technological destruction. It has always been difficult to see which has weighed more heavily in the balance.

Generation MM will take it for granted that people live longer, travel further, see more and have access to technologies unimaginable a few decades ago. They will recognise the technologies—because they take them for granted—as tools to make their lifestyles better, rather than as frightening determinants of their destinies. However, because the society in which they live will be so advanced technologically, they will value the natural, yearn for the wilderness and seek to refresh their lives from time to time by reconnecting with simple physical pleasures.

They will almost certainly have been at school longer than any previous generation. They will probably have studied the liberal arts rather than science and technology. While they may not have studied science and technology, they will have been using a computer terminal throughout most of their school lives and have had access to one in their home or local library. The home will be in a medium density housing development, with fibre optic cable provided to the door and communal gardens nearby.

They will have access to massive databases of information and will have seen films and video presentations with special effects that might make even Steven Spielberg gasp. They will be skilled in manipulating the words and images in these databases. Almost certainly they will focus on the immediate and the topical in the database. In many cases they will have little interest in history and will probably find it difficult to distinguish historical reality from myth.

They will have a high level of environmental awareness—recycling products and choosing environmentally sound products. But, faced with the wonders of a consumer society, they will reject extremist environmentalism which insists that they must go back to nature to save the world. They will know much about products and the companies which produce them because of their unparalleled access to information. They will be able to counterbalance the claims of advertising with the raw data on various Internet pages.

They will be used to economic insecurity and change. Their parents will have been scarred by the uncertainties of the late 20th century, just as their parents before them were scarred by the Great Depression and World War II. As a result they will be suspicious of rampant materialism and will look for ways to make society more co-operative and more decent. They will see the previous generation as lacking in values and direction and will regard standards, decency and values as important in politics, business and the community. They will be sceptical and at times downright cynical about business and government standards. Their access to technology will allow them to instantaneously identify breaches of such standards—wherever they occur in the world.

They themselves will be used to change. They will know that the nature of work alters and that they may have to change careers many times in their lives. They will understand that this will be made possible by a variety of core intellectual skills and competencies able to be adapted to different circumstances. They will insist that employers who expect top performance from them respect their abilities and their dignity—just as 19th century craftsmen took pride in *their* abilities.

They will probably speak English along with another language. They will think of themselves as part of the world, but will be proud of what defines them as unique individuals. They will dress casually to go to work and dress formally to go out. They may never visit a farm but will most probably have a pet. Balance and value will be important to them.

They will have been touched by the fervour of millenarianism and will be shaped by it—rejecting its extremes while subtly taking on some of the elements of its worldview.

Their Generation MM income will not be dependent on their gender, and they will feel comfortable about people on the basis of what they are like and how they behave rather than their colour, race or creed. They will respect minorities—such as white Anglo-Celts—and will even partake of much of their culture.

Being able to choose from a host of products and goods, they will look for value while taking it for granted that fun, colour and excitement are legitimate and everyday parts of life. Yet they will be moderate in much that they do. Having seen the extremes of the death of the old millennium and the birth of the new they will be suspicious of extremes—whether they be in politics, economics, religion or food.

They will have absorbed a spiritual element and will search in their technologically based world for sources of spiritual satisfaction. Their belief systems will be shaped by a paradoxical mix: technological competence; religious, New Age and millenarian myths; local patriotism; and unparalleled knowledge of the rest of the world. As a result, just when you think you've got them defined and categorised they will prove elusive by doing something unpredictable, and even seemingly irrational.

By about 2010 they will comprise the bulk of markets from which customers come; by 2020 they will shape the communities in which business will operate; and by 2030 they will be forming the governments which set the legislation and regulation under which business will operate. The decisions that the business world makes today will determine whether Generation MM consumes its products, sets out to work for its companies, agitates for laws to control its behaviour, allows it to prosper and grow.

FINDING THE MILLENNIUM EDGE

Drawing on the thoughts and advice of a wide range of people—management theorists and practitioners, economists, philosophers, sociologists, scientists and historians—I have sought to provide some insights into the confusing and paradoxical features of Generation MM and the new millennium.

At times in the next few years it will be difficult to view those confusing paradoxes calmly. The world will seem threatening and irrational. The new millennium will seem to be the start of a new age of uncertainty and fear. In such a situation there are no pat solutions or formulae which can guarantee success. But with foresight, insight and intelligence we can understand enough about what the new millennium means to allow us to avoid the disasters, to deal with the irrationality and to be optimistic that we have found the millennium edge.

We will have found the millennium edge when we close the gap between us and Generation MM—when we recognise that Generation MM and the 21st century *are* different and that we need different approaches to corporate cultures and structures; marketing and communication; and the relationships business forms with its communities and the world.

2 Society in the new millennium

A few years ago I was in a museum looking at a display on the evolution of humans. Staring at the model of a Neanderthal, I was struck by how different they appeared to be from us, when I had always imagined a sort of gradual evolution in which the various types of beings were probably more similar than different. Seeing the physical differences made it easy to understand that the Neanderthal lived a different lifestyle in a different environment.

The differences between the generation of today and Generation MM will not, of course, compare with those between us and the Neanderthal. The individual people who make up Generation MM will have much the same characteristics that have been present in people for centuries. While genetic engineering may be used to engineer out defects and prolong life, the genetic imperatives of life will remain. People will be motivated by the same desires for shelter, warmth and companionship as have driven people down through the centuries. They will look—even if perhaps dressed differently—the same as us.

The real knack in understanding Generation MM, however, lies in understanding that there will be profound differences in the social framework within which people search for and meet their basic desires. We must be careful that the outward similarities don't seduce us into making false assumptions about how much we might already be like what Generation MM will be.

In looking at society in the new millennium, I want to explore how Generation MM families will form, how religion will be important to attitudes, how attitudes to science, leisure, learning, the environment and social interaction will change, and how people will live. It is the differences in these areas that define the differences between 20th century society and the new millennium—between us and Generation MM.

The traditional family is dead! Long live its values and aspirations!

In a McDonalds store somewhere in Britain a separated family get together. A boy and his estranged parents meet at the store as they enjoy their McDonalds.

This sounds like real life—a marked contrast to the usual fare of advertising, the sort that features happy, traditional nuclear families having fun together. But it's not real life—it's a controversial television commercial.

In early 1995 McDonalds in the United Kingdom developed a new $65 million branding campaign. The scene I've just described was in one of the ads in a campaign which sought to take McDonalds advertising out of the nuclear family stereotype. The ad reflected the fact that single families now comprise 20 per cent of British families, and many industry observers applauded the campaign as a realistic new direction in British advertising.

But the Independent Television Commission received 60 complaints about the campaign. Many of them were realistic complaints suggesting that 'the apparently favourable outcome of the meeting could raise false hopes among children whose parents are separated'. But others were concerned that commercials should not deal with emotive issues such as separated families. A McDonalds spokesman said: 'We regret any offence but we believe the need for sensitivity was recognised'. The spokesman also confirmed that the company had no plans to use similar commercials in the future.

What happened here was that a company tried to reflect reality in its advertising—and was forced to retreat as a result.

The paradox this highlights is that the traditional nuclear family may be declining but its values still have to be accepted as the majority values. The irony of the McDonalds ad, of course, is that for decades social critics have been attacking advertising for creating unrealistic views of the world by depicting traditional Anglo nuclear families where the mother is a homemaker.

Reality is not a factor that often intrudes into debate about family policy. In the United States the Christian Right has three basic policy planks—for the family, for law and order and against abortion. Governments around the world spend hours and hours saying how committed they are to the family and its preservation.

Yet, while the rhetoric continues, the decline of the family continues. In the United States one in two marriages ends in divorce. In Australia one in three marriages ends in divorce. In the United Kingdom it is the same. The United States Bureau of Census claims the family is coming back because between 1990 and 1994 there was a rise of 510 000 in the number of two-parent families.

Yet there were only 25.1 million married couple families with children in the United States in 1994, compared with 9.9 million single mothers and 1.6 million single fathers. Single parenthood was growing at almost 4 per cent a year. In some inner urban United States neighbourhoods, it is estimated, only one in ten households with children has a father in residence. Three out of ten American children sleep in a different home from their fathers each night. And it has been estimated that up to 25 per cent of the British children of divorced families don't even know where their father lives.

Australian Bureau of Statistics (ABS) figures indicate that

the family comprising a married couple with children is not the common family formation. In Australia the numbers are:

• married and living with partner	6 620 495
• never married	3 844 578
• de facto	584 416
• separated but not divorced	374 142
• divorced	692 101
• widowed	829 737
• two-parent families with children	2 307 865
• couples without children	1 358 671
• one-parent families	552 412

But, despite the actual statistical reality of family life's significance to society, its emotional impact is still enormous. A United States survey, *The Loss of the American Dream,* found that families were the only category trusted more today than they were ten years ago.

Family life remains important to Australians as well. According to the Australian Bureau of Statistics (ABS), young single people aged between 15 and 24 and living with their families spend on average more than 50 per cent of their waking hours with their family members, and 40 per cent with friends. Older people average half their time with their family. Even young singles aged 15 to 24 and living *away* from their families average 16 hours a week (about 10 per cent of their time) visiting them. Of singles aged 25 to 59 who live alone, men spend 12 hours a week with family members and women 17 hours.

Despite the best efforts of the Christian Right and of various governments these trends are unlikely to change. Even in European countries with predominantly Catholic populations there are increases in the number of births out of wedlock and a higher incidence of unmarried couples living together.

In the 21st century people will continue to get married and will continue to have children. But a high proportion of those marriages will end in divorce and a high proportion of children will live in one-parent households. More gay and lesbian couples will be living together in arrangements regularised by some form of marriage contract supported by some form of legislatively provided framework. Many people will chose to live alone. With an ageing population, millions of lone women who have outlived their husbands will be in retirement homes or in some form of sole accommodation.

The nuclear family will have shifted, from being in decline, to the status of an unusual, minority household formation. Yet it is still unlikely that the impetus for family bonding will disappear. You might not be able to *choose* your family—as you can your friends and your partner—but the genetic ties that bind will still be strong. And in a worrying and troubled world the family will be the ultimate group around which you can draw a line. Anomalous or not, we need to learn to understand that an important factor shaping society will be a yearning for something which we spend most of our time destroying.

Religious fundamentalism is here. Believe me!

One of the most traditional parts of family life was the religious belief which underpinned it, legitimised it and shaped it. Yet for much of the late 20th century it appeared that this was changing, as secularism was progressively winning its centuries-old war with religion.

The victory appeared to be more a product of attrition than anything else. For many, the World War I trenches and the World War II concentration camps killed off the concept of God. But in the 1950s and 1960s it appeared that religion was losing ground simply because of boredom and loss of relevance. By the 1980s it would have been almost a cause for headlines if an Anglican Archbishop revealed that he actually believed in God and the literal Resurrection.

Yet religion has made a huge resurgence—particularly in

the form of devout faith and religious fundamentalism. Born-again Christians; people who believe in the literal truth of the Bible or the Koran; and, most importantly, people to whom religion is fundamental to their lives, are now common in a society which had appeared to be becoming more secular. Christopher Hitchens in his book *Missionary Position*[6] recounts how the British broadcaster and writer Malcolm Muggeridge was making a film about Mother Teresa. The cameraman was reluctant to shoot one interior scene because it appeared to be too dark. However, he had some new Eastman Kodak film stock which was said to perform very well in low light conditions. He decided to film, but had little hope that it would be successful. When the film was processed the scene glowed with a wonderful light. Muggeridge declared it was a miracle and that the light was a mystical sign of Mother Teresa's saintliness.

Since then the story has been repeated many times that Mother Teresa's saintliness can light the dark. But we know today that it was really a technical miracle accomplished by the wonders of Eastman Kodak's film. Today it is doubtful if the reality will ever triumph over the miraculous myth. It is unlikely that Kodak would be foolish enough to appear to sully a saint in order to make a point about its film, the photographer is resigned to having the story told in the Muggeridge version, and Muggeridge has gone on—to discover whether he or the heathen were right.

During the 1980s there was ongoing debate about the Turin Shroud. It had been known for centuries that the shroud was not what was claimed but, during the resurgence of religious spirit, serious people and serious magazines produced serious arguments about this wondrous piece of cloth. Finally, modern carbon testing confirmed what the church had already known. Whether it made any difference to people's belief is a moot point, to say the least.

Religious revival is real. More than 90 per cent of Americans believe in God. Some 70 per cent believe in the Devil. The former Republican Presidential candidate, Pat Robertson, and allegedly Ronald Reagan himself, believe in the coming of Armageddon—the fulfilment of the prophecies of the Book of Revelation. About 40 per cent of Americans believe that nuclear fire will bring Armageddon and lead to Rapture in which the godly will live in eternal happiness. Jerry Falwell, an influential member of the moral majority and Christian Right so important in American politics, believes in an imminent Second Coming and the advent of the millennium.

It is difficult to imagine Thomas Jefferson—perhaps the greatest public figure in American history and one of the most cultured political leaders the world has seen—being elected President today. As a deist with real doubts about Christianity, he might well be unelectable.

The impact on American politics is seen in many ways. In 1995 the Presidential candidate Senator Dole found it necessary to attack the Disney company for distributing a film, *Priest,* about a homosexual priest. Dole is apparently an intelligent, witty and rather sardonic man, but he found it necessary to take a position he almost certainly didn't believe in so as to pacify the religious fundamentalists. Ironically, it turned out that his wife had shares in the Disney company, and that shareholding became one of the non-crisis sensations with which the United States media is filled.

The United States has always been a godly place—its earliest European settlers were largely refugees from religious persecution who wanted to set up societies in which they could persecute those who disagreed with them. But the United States is now no exception in the spread of religion around the world.

Australia is one of the most secular and sybaritic societies imaginable—beaches, food, brown bodies and sun combine to create a nation of leisure worshippers. Yet, of the 18 million Australians, only 2.2 million told the 1991 Census collectors that they didn't believe in God. In Australia, according to the Bureau of Statistics, Catholics have overtaken Anglicans as the biggest faith in the past decade (due to migration from Vietnam, the Philippines and South America), but Muslims, Buddhists and Pentecostals are the fastest growing religions. The approximate number of people in each faith is as follows:

- Catholic 4 607 000
- Anglican 4 019 000
- Uniting 1 388 000
- Presbyterian 732 000

- Orthodox 475 000
- Baptist 280 000
- Lutheran 251 000
- Pentecostal 151 000
- Muslim 148 000
- Buddhist 140 000
- Church of Christ 78 000
- Jehovah's Witness 75 000
- Judaism 74 000
- Atheist (don't believe in God) 2 177 000

In the past few decades the Western media have been filled with stories about Muslim fundamentalism sweeping the world. But Christian fundamentalism is also growing apace. For example, by 1992 there were over 1000 independent Christian sects in Africa, many of them exhibiting fundamentalist traits.

Besides the rise of fundamentalist religions there has been an explosion in the quasi-religions associated with the New Age. Many a green prays for environmental deliverance as fervently as does the religious sect member who longs for Armageddon to transport all the godly to heaven—and consign the rest of us to a final reckoning with Satan. Equally, there are greens who espouse belief systems very similar to the animist religions of Africa and Latin America.

In Asian societies, traditional religions and ways of life—Islam, Hinduism, Buddhism, Taoism, Confucianism, feng-shui—are all still highly important.

Yet most Western middle class people—the sort that make up the managerial class in most companies—still get embarrassed talking about religion. Indeed, they are more likely to feel comfortable talking about the frequency of orgasm in their marital sex life than they are their spiritual life. But in the 21st century they will be dealing with a society that takes religion seriously . . . a society that even believes in millenarianism and various forms of Armageddon. If they ignore that new religious spirit they will surely end in the corporate hell to which business failures are condemned.

Perception as reality; myth more real than fact

Side by side with religious revivalism is a resurgence in belief in myths. The resurgence is due both to the need for myth to enliven life and the need for myth to explain our lives.

There is a Chinese fortune cookie which says: 'We do not see things the way they are; we see them the way we are'. In other words, we shape what we see through the filter of our attitudes. In a millenarian age this trend is most pronounced—so pronounced that it is often difficult for people to distinguish between myth and reality. Indeed, to many people their perception *is* the reality.

How we perceive and understand things in the Western world is very much the product of our history. From the advent of Christianity through to the Reformation there was really only one way of seeing things—from the viewpoint of the one universal church. Heretics may have disagreed, but the dominant way of seeing the world was within this religious prism. With the Reformation this universal view of the world began to break down and it became possible to approach the truth from different viewpoints. The individual religions which emerged after the Reformation may have been as intolerant of dissent as the one universal church, but the reality was that there was now more than one truth on offer. The Enlightenment brought an even more massive change in how we see things. The Enlightenment basically said there were many ways—rational ways—to approach the truth. In the 20th century we have moved on a step. Quantum mechanics and postmodernism have challenged the very idea of truth, arguing that there are many truths which largely depend on your standpoint at the time.

In the new millennium people will inherit the impact of this view of life—this belief that what you perceive is what is real. Indeed, in many cases the unreal will be more real and exciting than the real!

Over the past two millennia a number of factors, conscious and unconscious, have contributed to this situation. Symbol and myth have always played a role in our life. Aby Warburg, the German art historian and a member of the famous banking family, saw symbols as an integral part of everyone's lives. Sir James Frazer, author of the *Golden Bough*[8] and a pioneering anthropologist, argued that symbols were a primitive hangover from the past. He saw symbolism and myth in conflict with post-Enlightenment and rationality. We need not debate the point. Symbol and myth are part of life regardless of whether they are an integral element or just some primeval hangover from our past.

Symbols and myths are important in part because we live in societies which are constantly creating new symbols and myths. In the United States Halloween is now a $2.4 billion industry—bigger than both Easter and Thanksgiving. *The Economist* of 28 October 1995 said: 'What was once a Celtic festival for the dead is now chiefly an occasion for middle-aged Americans to summon up their memories of childhood'. An opportunity, in other words, to relive a mythical childhood when the streets were safe and life was fun. And so the adults prance in the streets from house to house, play trick or treat, and dramatically increase the demand for pumpkins!

Halloween has become what is known as an invented tradition—now a part of American and even Australian culture—which is seen to be strongly traditional but is sometimes of quite recent origin. Christmas, as we celebrate it today, is largely a 19th century invention. The Kwanza African-American festival and Chanukah—a Jewish festival near Christmas—are recently invented traditions. The best discussion of such invented traditions is to be found in the book *The Invention of Tradition.*[9] The book is a collection of essays about traditions and how they came about. For instance, the tradition of British monarchical pomp and circumstance was invented largely in the early 20th century. There had been no huge fuss about coronations and royal ritual until Edwardian times, when it was felt that the British monarchy must be made to appear more magnificent than competitor monarchies in

Europe. The book also shows that the famous Scottish tartans we see today—and much of the so-called Highland tradition—are a 19th century English invention.

Some of the traditions that have been created are, of course, based on conscious attempts by the political classes of a particular era to create a certain image of the society. As early as 1912 a French historian, Collas, remarked that much of the activity undertaken by the court of the French king Louis XIV resembled publicity activity. Serious historians didn't pursue the point until the 1970s and 1980s, when a leading historian, Natalie Zemon Davis,[10] began the intensive study of the role of ritual in royal courts. Her work prompted a younger generation of historians to look afresh at traditional views of royalty and royal communication.

Two of the best of these young historians, Lisa Jardine and Peter Burke, have written important books which look at communication by two key historical figures, Erasmus and Louis XIV, through the prism of modern public relations and communication techniques.

Peter Burke's book *The Fabrication of Louis XIV*[11] sets out to contribute to 'the history of communication, the history of production, circulation and reception of symbolic forms'—in essence, how the king's 'image' was created and enhanced. The word 'fabrication' that appears in the title of the book is used in its traditional sense of building and constructing, rather than in the more modern pejorative sense. In this context his book is about constructing image.

Burke recounts how Louis and his advisers worked systematically to combine a variety of contemporary communication techniques in order to shape the king's image. The tools used included printed materials, architectural decorations, paintings, medallions, ballets, operas, court rituals and other forms of spectacle. Third party endorsements were fostered through the establishment of institutions which undertook studies and issued pronouncements on the events of the reign.

Lisa Jardine's book is about a man considered by many to be the greatest intellectual of the last thousand years—Erasmus, the great Low Countries humanist. In *Erasmus Man of Letters*[12] Jardine tells us how a man considered the personification of goodness, truth and virtue set about promoting and burnishing his image. She describes her book as 'a story of extraordinarily complex and sophisticated manipulations of writing and printing designed to construct a worldwide reputation for both a movement (Low Countries humanism) and an individual'.

Interestingly, one can view American history through a similar prism.

Some years ago, speaking on political lobbying, I observed that the Boston Tea Party was a classic example of a public relations event used to shape public opinion and generate publicity. The participants got dressed up in costumes. They took direct action by boarding a ship. They made a symbolic gesture—emptying the tea into Boston harbour. And they warned the media in advance of their plans. It had all the features of the best sort of media event—newsworthiness, strong visual material and all held on a quiet news day.

John Budd, ex-President of the Public Relations Society of America, recently used David Hackett Fisher's book on Paul Revere[13] to illustrate that Revere was not the lone rider of myth but a person who was mobilising a 'painstakingly developed communication network of local citizen leaders'. He targeted opinion leaders in churches and other organisations. To follow up, the revolutionaries quickly produced eyewitness accounts of the battles at Lexington and Concord and disseminated them widely to raise awareness of the revolutionary cause.

What is clear is that for many hundreds of years we have been blurring the distinctions between myth and reality.

Before we scoff, and say that such manipulation and belief in myth would not survive in the cynical 20th century, we should be aware of the extent to which the daily media play a role in further blurring myth and reality. It is now commonplace for some newspapers and television stations to report on characters in soap operas as if they were real. In other words, they not only devote pages to the latest love lives of the actors but also report developments in the soap opera plots as if they too were real. By the end of the massive worldwide promotion of the question 'Who shot J.R.?' that particular soap opera character had had more coverage than some of the four assassinated United States presidents. Imagine walking down a

US street and asking 100 people to name all the assassinated presidents and then asking them to name the J.R. soap opera. Ponder for a moment what the outcome might be.

In recent years there have been a bevy of books about the other side of media myth creation—the extent to which the media create unreal agendas, peddle untruths and encourage the dissemination of myth. Five recent books illustrate the situation. Paul Weaver[14] argues that news coverage is so obsessed with sensationalism and phoney crises that what is reported is totally distorted to the point of being a 'culture of lying'. In *Toxic Sludge is Good for You*[15] John Stauber and Sheldon Rampton recount dozens of public relations campaigns that manipulated the truth—with the assistance of the media. Susan Trento's work[16] describes how one public relations firm created false news through a Congressional Committee in order to further the cause of the Kuwaiti royal family. Other case studies of activities run by the same firm are given in the book. *Tainted Truth: The Manipulation of Fact in America*[17] by Cynthia Crossen looks at the impact of innumeracy on reporting and shows how doubtful data are used to shape policy. In *Who Stole the News?* Mort Rosenblum[18] tells us how foreign correspondents fail to communicate social realities—preferring to report on natural disasters.

The whole problem is compounded by the proliferation of media and media images. In Beirut, during the civil war, young gunmen watched Rambo movies and fired at the cinema ceiling with machine-guns. At home, on any given night, people have a steady diet of news, commercials and entertainment in which it is difficult to distinguish the individual ingredients. The entertainment features the products; and in the commercials the entertainers endorse the products.

People look back to the past as a golden age. After the horrors of World War I the English looked back on Edwardian England as being warmer, happier and more peaceful. Climatic records show that it *was*, in fact, warmer than the immediate postwar period—but also the nation was racked by strikes over trade unions, by suffragettes and by the Irish question. And a generation of historians tried to convince the world that the pre–Industrial Revolution period was a pastoral paradise. Some environmentalists today are still trying to do the same, despite the obvious advances in health and standards of living that the Industrial Revolution made possible. The whole concept of 'noble savages' in Eden-like wildernesses is another manifestation of this yearning for an imagined past. It is even arguable that the glorious days of economic growth and stable family life in the United States were either not true or just an aberration confined to the 1950s.

In the new millennium the millenarians will have their version of reality. The media will bombard Generation MM with dozens of other versions. We will all have our perceptions shaped by events, prejudices and attitudes from the old millennium. In many cases myth will merge into reality. If we fail to recognise that—and assume that everyone is rational, or able to distinguish between myth and reality—we will fail to understand what is really shaping people's attitudes.

'None of the younger generation can read', we cry . . . and yet . . .

The managers of today are probably the last management generation to be brought up on the products of traditional print technology diets. We studied books at school and universities. We read newspapers—and we imagine that others still do. We respect the written word.

Yet, in the totality of human existence, printing has not been around for very long. In medieval times people learnt through pictures. That's why medieval cathedrals were covered with carvings, and that's why Passion Plays were performed. A largely illiterate population was educated through images. In primeval times, when prehistoric people sought to express themselves, they did it in images—in cave paintings and by covering their bodies with ochre.

From the late 15th century onwards the Gutenberg revolution in printing technology revolutionised the Western world. The spread of compact, mass-produced information parcels—books—opened up new areas of inquiry and led to the spread of literacy.

In the late 20th century it was fashionable to say that we had seen the end of the Gutenberg Age. The Canadian media theorist Marshall McLuhan[19] saw the new information era as a post-Gutenberg age. Images and new forms of information were going to transform the world. To an extent, McLuhan and likeminded theorists were right. There was an information explosion and there has now been an explosion of new media and new means of communication. In the next millennium this trend will accelerate rather than diminish.

But the surprising thing about all this change is the way it has persuaded many people to conclude that the world is suffering a literacy crisis. We are told day in and day out that television, computers, video games and so on are rotting the minds of the young. We're told that the young don't read and that even their magazines are full of images and not words. They spend hours in front of screens at home, and at school they are deprived of the great works of literature thanks to soft option courses, theme studies and a series of politically correct comic book windows on life. There is an element of truth in this. And it is not just literacy in the narrow sense. Some African-Americans are fed educational pap in which 'blackness' is held to be the root of all culture. Some white Americans who are taught about their country's 1917–1918 and the 1942–1945 wars are a little unsure as to who the Western allies during those wars actually were and where Europe actually is! In some Australian schools, children emerge barely able to read after 12 years of schooling and with little or no knowledge about their nation's history and its system of government. While concerns about literacy exist, fewer students are claimed to be studying science and mathematics, and innumeracy is also alleged to be a problem. In at least one Australian State, Victoria, there is apparently also an acute shortage of science and mathematics teachers.

Part of this concern is created by the never-ending cycle of intergenerational conflict. To the young, the older generation are hopeless and outmoded. To the old, the younger generation are useless and not maintaining standards. This intergenerational conflict is only natural.

I was staggered, in the office the other day, to discover that one of our younger staff wasn't too sure who Cromwell was, and thought his name was Arthur and not Oliver. *She* was staggered to discover that I didn't know who Claudia Schiffer was. Initially this was just further evidence for the mature that the young read nothing, and for the young that the old know nothing. But quickly we realised that the real lesson was about how we could learn from each other. You and I will return to this lesson when we consider corporate structures for the new millennium, in Chapter 9.

Another part of the concern is created by a lack of awareness of the continuing role of print. Paper production and books are going to continue to play significant roles in the economies and cultures of many countries. The book is a compact and convenient way to package and transmit information. Rising literacy rates in emerging economies are making huge demands on educational and entertainment texts.

But the real lesson for the next millennium is that the trends demonstrate that the new generation is developing new ways to acquire, use and manipulate knowledge.

Computer-literate Generation MM members are able to access databanks of a wider range than the student of yesterday studying in a local library could ever imagine. They are able to work with images, graphs, texts and sound to produce presentations of magnificent sophistication. They take for granted the pace and innovation of music videos.

Standards of education at the later stages of secondary school and the earlier stages of tertiary education are higher than ever before. More and more young people around the world are participating in tertiary education. More and more people are acquiring new skills. If this were not so our economies would not be in the process of being transformed from economies in which musclepower was important to ones in which knowledge is important.

No young manager today laboriously writes out a report

in longhand, asks a secretary to type it up and then edits it in pen. Almost no young manager would be courageous enough to ask a personal assistant to take dictation—now recognised as a demeaning and inefficient way to produce typed material. Most have superior keyboard, spreadsheet and other skills which enable them to function self-sufficiently almost anywhere in the world. Every day they are finding new ways to manipulate data and images to enable them to communicate them in new and more effective ways.

And significant numbers of them still read books for leisure!

In the new millennium we will need to understand this shift in competencies and emphasis. We must gear up our communications to deal with the new reality. And we have to stop bleating like old fogies about the declining standards of education and literacy, and realise that it may well be the old who need to catch up and improve their skills.

Workaholics will walk the dog

In the past few years a constant topic of conversation has been what long hours people work. In the good old days, the odd Friday lunch became an all-afternoon affair and an early end to the day on Friday was not unusual. Today, people—even in quite junior jobs—are at work before 8.00 a.m. and leave well after 6.00 p.m. Lunch is normally a hurried sandwich at the desk and alcohol at lunchtime is a rare event indeed—except in the more civilised European parts of the world.

According to *Fortune* magazine of 15 September 1995 two-thirds of Americans—more than 75 million—work other than the traditional nine to five day. Senior executives now regularly work the dawn to dusk shift that has always been common among peasants in the fields. Between 1975 and 1995 the average hours at work for Americans went from 43.1 to 50.6, with the hours devoted to leisure declining from 24.3 to 19.2.

The trend for those in jobs is clearly to longer hours, shorter holidays, more work-related activities and less leisure.

An American advertising agency, Bozell Worldwide, carried out a 1995 study for *United States News and World Report* on how Americans saw their quality of life. They found that leisure time is now more valuable than money to half of the population. Only 35 per cent of those surveyed would prefer more money if it required more time at work. Only 1 per cent nominated work in answer to a question about spending a few hours of free time. The top priorities for the respondents were family life, spiritual life and health. Some 70 per cent of them said they felt stress during the workday—30 per cent a lot of stress and 40 per cent some stress. There was also a huge sense of loss and decline, with only 29 per cent believing their children would have a better quality of life than they now have.

And when people take leisure it is hurriedly or packaged in form. In holiday seasons airports are packed with travellers and children. Beaches are not havens but masses of baking humanity. People 'do' London, Prague or wherever in a few days of whirlwind travel and rushing from cathedral to gallery to museum to shops. The ultimate package holiday is at a theme park or a Club Med, where the traveller rarely has to venture outside the envelope the leisure packager provides.

Non-travel leisure is often almost industrialised. The jogger or aerobics person needs the right shoes, the right timeslot, the right centre. They accept pain for gain as readily as the stress at work. Young adults engage in organised leisure through team sports, movies and music. Older people bowl or play golf, using expensive equipment and wearing fashionable clothes. The only passive leisure activities are reading, watching television and spending time with the family—and television takes the bulk of this time. In the case of Australians it is four hours of viewing each day for 95 per cent of those aged 15 and over.

In short, leisure is becoming almost as stressful as work.

In the 21st century some members of Generation MM are

going to ask that the treadmill be stopped. They will discover that the fusion of work, life and leisure has unbalanced their existence and deprived them of pleasure. Everywhere they turn in order to escape will be just one more part of the problem. In the end they will discover that there is an alternative: a non-stressful form of exercise, a chance for contemplation or polite discussion, an opportunity to see things differently than from the business class seat of a jet—and an opportunity to meet new people.

Every morning I try to get up early. Pull on a tracksuit and walk down to the beach and then through the streets. See other walkers—who smile, where joggers grimace—and see subtle changes to houses, gardens and shops. My head clears, my body relaxes without being pounded and tortured . . . and I often have my best ideas. At weekends I walk with my wife and the pace dictates the pace of our conversation. Instead of hurried words, scrawled messages and telephone calls, we actually talk.

That's why this wonderful alternative—the old-fashioned, cost-free walk—is the only leisure activity that can probably never be industrialised. Exactly the same phenomenon—getting back in touch with a different rhythm of life—is achieved by those who walk the dog or play with a pet animal. In this case it is not only a form of non-industrialised leisure but is also one way, in an increasingly urbanised society, to begin to reintegrate ourselves with something very important. Let's look at this.

For thousands upon thousands of years almost every human lived in close contact with nature. Thousands of years ago society survived on the basis of hunting and gathering, with the occasional hunting trip providing major quantities of game and the staple diet being derived from gathering fruits, berries and other foods. Then, up until just a century ago, the vast majority of the world's population worked in the fields, where the change of season dictated the tasks and the diet of daily life. But the pattern had begun to change in the late 18th century, with the Industrial Revolution. Much later—in the mid–20th century—the Green Revolution dramatically increased crop yields, and agribusiness started to replace the small family farm. The population shift from country to city accelerated.

Today the world is being transformed into a world of towns, cities and mega-cities. The once giant metropolises of New York and London have been dwarfed by Mexico City, Rio de Janeiro, Sao Paulo, Beijing and a range of other cities in emerging economies. In Australia, five cities—Sydney, Melbourne, Brisbane, Perth and Adelaide—contain 60 per cent of the population. Another 11 per cent live in cities with populations of more than 100 000.

Whereas once most families around the world had contact with at least a small plot of land, either leased or their own, the standard form of accommodation is becoming the suburban house, apartment or slum dwelling.

In all countries a few of the better off compensate by buying farmlets or country retreats. The former British Prime Minister, Harold Wilson, once bought himself a country house. Asked how he, as a socialist, justified owning a country house, he replied that his definition of socialism was when everyone owned a country house. But the mathematics and geography of the modern world make the likelihood of rural retreats reactivating people's links with the soil about as achievable as Wilson's plan.

Yet our increasing urbanisation is relatively recent. Even by the new millennium there will be many people who can remember when they had contact with the land or who have family in the country somewhere. More importantly, we still have strong primeval urges—dating back to the earliest days of our evolution—which link us to life in the wild. And one of the most important of the links is that with animals.

The traditional view has been that people's relationship with animals in prehistoric times was basically that of hunter to hunted. It was believed that a few animals were domesticated—dogs and cattle to begin with—while farming was being developed. But an Australian scientist, David Paxton, has suggested that, rather than domesticating the dog, we actually evolved in co-operation with the dog—that people and dogs in prehistoric times were mutually supportive, providing each other with assistance while hunting and with warmth and mutual protection. There is no doubt that in many prehistoric sites there is clear evidence of the links between people and dogs. Whether Paxton is right or not, it is clear that the bonding with animals has been an important part of human life for an extremely long time.

This primeval need—allied with increasing urbanisation—is going to make the human/companion-animal bond even more important in the 21st century. Already people's pets are important. According to a 1995 *United States News and World Report/CNN Poll,* 60 per cent of Americans say that owning a pet leads to a more satisfying life.

The challenge in the new millennium will be to find ways to ensure that people can still enjoy the benefits of pet ownership despite the changing nature of our built environment. It may be that governments and the medical profession will need to encourage even wider pet ownership to protect individuals and societies from the stresses of uncertain existence. At the very least, we will need to develop new urban planning codes, new ways of designing buildings and new ways to help people achieve the benefits of responsible pet ownership.

Prehistoric people huddled in their caves seeking warmth and protection from their families—and, it now appears, their dogs as well. Many Generation MMers will be huddling in a new form of cave—high rise apartments and housing complexes. We need to realise that they too will huddle with a pet—a companion—which will provide them with the same sort of protection in a new millennium as the pet did in prehistoric days.

And they will walk the dog when they need an antidote to the stresses of their work and responsibilities.

The surprising thing nevertheless is that, despite these pressures and strains of long hours and life in general, we will still be better off in many respects. Better off because of the profound technical changes that the new millennium will inherit from our century.

Science, superstition and the New Age

Have you lived longer than either of your great-grandparents? Have you had pneumonia, or some other once life-threatening disease, miraculously cured by an antibiotic? Have you travelled across the Pacific or the Atlantic in less than a day? If so you are a living illustration of the fact that the 20th century has been remarkable for the achievements of science in almost every field of human endeavour.

We live longer, we travel faster and we have greater levels of comfort. Yet it is becoming increasingly obvious that the new millennium is seeing the re-emergence of superstitions which once had been banished by rationalism. In the year 412 a Christian mob in Alexandria murdered Hypatia in a bid to end 'pagan' science and replace it with a new emphasis on religious dogma. From then until the days of Bacon and the Enlightenment, science had to battle against superstition. For a few hundred years it seemed that science was winning. Today the battle is being fought again.

Now 'New Agers' offer a new mysticism and a rejection of rationality. They want to abolish the Enlightenment, attack the rationality of science and technology and replace it with new belief systems. Around the Western world there are people—otherwise totally normal and rational—who believe in astrology and buy astrology books. Others read the tarot cards. Some believe that people give off visible auras. In Australia there is a political party—the Natural Law Party—which wants to remedy the world's problems through rediscovering the natural laws that, it says, underpin society. In Victoria it promised to resolve the State public transport deficit by means of meditation! While some cynics argued that its policy was no more pointless than those pursued by the major political parties, it does appear to require an even greater suspension of disbelief than listening to politicians normally does.

The Gaia theory of the environment—in its most extreme manifestations—is an example of a New Age approach that claims to be an all-embracing theory of everything. A bestselling novel by Umberto Eco, *Foucalt's Pendulum*,[20] was based on a group of friends in a publishing firm bringing together a vast variety of conspiracy theories in one giant computer program. The important things about the book were that it was based on Eco's own experiences in being asked to publish hundreds of books on New Age themes; and that few readers actually recognised that it was a comedy.

The *New England Journal of Medicine* has stated that in 1990 Americans made 425 million visits to unconventional healers—compared with 388 million visits to doctors. Faith healing, homoeopathy and a host of other remedies are preferred to penicillin and other products of science. There is no doubt that the world could well learn from traditional remedies. Herbal treatments obviously have some efficacy and many modern medical interventions are costly and unproductive. But the New Agers don't just recommend that alternatives should be considered. They go further. They reject the scientific ground and proclaim that the alternatives are not only superior but the only real option.

In an uncertain world the millenarian fantasies are able to feed on these New Age beliefs and superstitions. They appeal to the spiritual cravings of Generation MM. One of the heroes of the Eastern European velvet revolution was the current Czech President, Vaclav Havel. A playwright and a courageous anti-communist, he is probably the world's most civilised and liberal head of state. His views on international relations and domestic policy have been marked by vision, decency and profound commonsense. Yet, when asked to ponder the spiritual and the scientific, he immediately distrusts the scientific. Speaking in 1994 at a Fourth of July public meeting at the Independence Hall in Philadelphia, he said: 'We may know immeasurably more about the universe than our ancestors did, and yet it increasingly seems that they knew something more essential about it than we do, something that escapes us'.

Here, from one of the world's most outstanding individuals, in one sentence, we see both the assertion of the limits of the scientific and the notion of a mystical alternative.

The mysticism—linked with newly religious feelings—is part of the search for values and part of the search for comforting explanations in uncertain times. The most remarkable thing about human beings is that they are purposeful, even though they have developed a scientific system which has enabled them to comprehend that they are an insignificant speck of dust in a seemingly infinite universe. But because we are purposeful we find it difficult to believe that there is no purpose beyond those provided by our genes and survival instincts. There has to be something more, some further explanation. New Age mysticism is just one of the responses to this paradox. Distrust of technology is another. A 1987 National Science Foundation survey found that 41 per cent of Americans worried about the impact of technology on moral values and a similar number wanted restraints on technology.

The anti-scientific bent extends to the schoolroom. In classes in Victoria an official environmental curriculum included the assertion: 'population + technology = pollution'. An essentially irrational and unscientific message was presented in mathematical format as if to convey some new, higher reality. While the statement is clearly nonsense as a formula, a generation of school children have been taught that it is a 'fact' as accurate as the trigonometric formulae they are taught.

Another manifestation of this general problem is people's difficulty in understanding risk. They blithely drive cars, ride motorcycles and cross roads. Yet they worry about flying in aeroplanes, and are readily persuaded that a substance is carcinogenic when the risk factor is actually infinitesimal.

The concept of parts per million or parts per billion is also poorly understood. In Victoria, Environment Protection Authority licence forms require companies to list every discharge element—however small. There are, as a result, headings for heavy metals such as mercury. Today economic reality, let alone environmental responsibility, would dissuade companies from discharging heavy metals. But in many processes it is inevitable that there will be traces of heavy metals, just as there are traces in the soil in our gardens. A company in Victoria some years ago was severely embarrassed when a local environmental group obtained a copy of its waste discharge licence and issued a media release to the local media saying that the company was dumping heavy metals into the local river. The evidence—that traces were listed on the licence. The local newspaper ran the story despite attempts to explain to them that the so-called heavy metal pollution was merely traces of elements in about the same quantities that are found in a can of beer. Science and reality lost, and superstition won, because neither the group nor the journalist had the basic mathematical skills to realise that it was the allegation and not the discharge that was scandalous.

It should be said, nevertheless, that part of this New Age suspicion of science has been brought about by scientists themselves. For years doctors have basked in a godlike aura which, they felt, removed the need to explain what they were doing and why. Surgeons routinely recommend surgical practices with failure rates so high that, if they were pharmaceuticals, would have had the responsible regulatory body banning their use.

Scientists—some of them, admittedly, burnt by excursions into the media or other public forums—communicate poorly. Other scientists are simply arrogant about their role and the role of the community. In her fascinating autobiography, *Breakfast with Beaverbrook*[21], the Australian historian Ann Moyal tells how she once wrote a major analysis of the Australian Atomic Energy Commission. Published in the ANZAAS journal, *Search*, it said: 'Throughout [its history] there was insufficient opportunity for public debate and little for assessment and meaningful comment among the scientific and public communities. Overall there was a disdain for public accountability on the part of a major scientific establishment'. The former AAEC chairman, Sir Phillip Baxter, replied to Moyal's analysis:

> Our technological civilisation produces a continuing stream of problems of a most complex technical character. Only a small proportion of the population is capable of understanding issues of the sort, even if they were to make the effort. Many elected representatives, though not all, are in the same situation. The experts must in the end be trusted. To submit such matters to the ballot box, the street demonstration or the politician who has a divine conviction that

> he understands technical problems, can only lead to trouble and possible disaster.

A quarter of a century later some scientists are still saying 'trust us'—and the Generation MM New Agers are asking 'why?'. In the new millennium, when what is superstitious will appear to be scientific, explaining the reality will be one of business's biggest challenges.

Environmental awareness is here to stay

In many international magazines you will see a striking image of a young Eurasian woman in a hard hat and holding a clipboard. The photograph captures youth, beauty and intelligence. Alongside the photograph are the words: 'Does your environmental policy meet your granddaughter's expectations?'

It's the image and the headline on a Waste Management International advertisement. The advertisement reads:

> Is your business or community among the millions of customers across the world already using our environmental services? If it is, you'll be aware of our total commitment to protecting and sustaining the environment. Why? Because we believe a high standard of performance is good for the environment and essential to maintain the public trust and the confidence of our customers and investors.

The ad epitomises the new environmental reality. For a few brief moments in the 1980s it appeared that the environmental tidal wave would pass, and life would get back to normal. While the crescendo of environmental debate has passed, community awareness has simply reached a new plateau.

Indeed, in Australia a 1995 ABS survey showed that seven out of ten people were concerned with at least one specific environmental problem. And a US Nuclear Energy Institute 'Perspective on Public Opinion' survey, reported in the Institute's newsletter in July 1995, showed that most Americans think of themselves as environmentalists: 79 per cent say they would use that term to describe themselves at least 'a little', and 20 per cent 'a lot'. Among Americans overall, preserving natural resources is an extremely important issue (87 per cent) and 32 per cent deem it the most urgent issue threatening the environment. Four in five (82 per cent) say that reducing air pollution/greenhouse gases is an extremely important issue; 29 per cent say it is the most urgent matter. Assuring a reliable supply of electricity is called very important by 80 per cent, but only 6 per cent say it is the most urgent issue.

Some years ago I was asked to speak at a conference in Toronto on the history of environmentalism and what it taught us about the environmental tidal wave encompassing communities. With only a limited amount of research, I quickly discovered that much of the environmental debate was neither new nor particularly surprising. Environmentalists have been concerned for more than a century about many of the same issues that dominate newspaper headlines today. If we take into account the Roman Senate's concern about Rome's chariot traffic problem, environmentalism can be said to be two millennia old.

But the most significant indicator of growing environmental concern was the creation of the United Kingdom's National Society for Clean Air. (We know all about London smog, thanks to 19th century novels and Sherlock Holmes films!) Smoke abatement legislation was passed in Britain as early as 1273, and there was a commission of inquiry into air pollution in 1307 in response to widespread community concern. The year before that a man was executed for burning sea-coal in London.

After the Industrial Revolution the problem became acute. In 1898 the artist Sir William Richmond wrote to *The Times* urging action. The next year the Coal Smoke Abatement Society was established, with committee members including the Duke of Westminster, Viscount Middleton and the famous chemist Lord Kelvin. This is perhaps the origin of three well-known tactics to draw attention to environmental problems: generate publicity; form a group; and get some famous individuals to endorse your case.

In 1905 the Society's treasurer invented the word 'smog' as a means of describing the smoke/fog problem they were fighting—providing us with an early example of attention-grabbing terms that fit neatly in a headline.

Over the next 45 years the Society used a host of techniques with which we are familiar today. Smoke inspectors made independent checks on chimneys and reported offences to the sanitary authorities—an obvious precedent for the Greenpeace raids of today! Major international conferences were held; draft legislation was prepared; evidence was submitted to parliamentary inquiries; and considerable publicity was generated.

The culmination of this campaigning came on Thursday 4 December 1952, when climatic conditions created one of the worst smogs in British history. Over the next three days more than 4000 died from heart and lung disease. There had been similar incidents internationally in Belgium in 1930 and in Pennsylvania in 1948, but publicity about the 1952 tragedy spread around the world.

By 1956 the government had introduced a comprehensive Clean Air Act. Significantly, while it had taken 683 years to get from 1273 to the 1956 UK legislation, most other Western nations introduced similar legislation within the next decade.

This illustrates further important lessons about environmental politics. First, that real pollution problems can only be fixed by real anti-pollution action. Second, that if it's an issue in one part of the globe it is inevitable that it will become an issue elsewhere. Third, the speed at which it happens is always increasing, simply because of technological change and the globalisation of communications.

A second indicator of growing environmental concern is the way the evolution of urban planning has been linked to the environment. The focal point for 20th century debate about planning has probably been the garden city concept—the idea of creating suburbs which incorporate gardens, sensible layouts and all the infrastructure that we need in order to keep a modern society functioning.

Ostensibly the garden city idea emanated from Sir Ebenezer Howard, a British reformer of the late 19th and early 20th centuries, who sought to reverse the trend occurring from rural towards urban life. He founded two garden cities and inspired others in the United Kingdom and Australia as well as similar developments throughout the world.

But the concept really grew from the intellectual impact of the socialist reformer William Morris—a serious candidate for the title of founder of the modern Green movement. Morris wrote, talked, designed and inspired people to follow what was called the arts and crafts movement. Essentially it was an attempt—in a rapidly industrialising society—to recapture pre-industrial production and societal modes. His utopian text, *News from Nowhere*, portrays Britain as a land from which factories, pollution and urban sprawl have been eradicated and where cities have become small village-like clusters surrounded by trees and gardens. This vision, set out more than 100 years ago, is remarkably similar to the vision articulated by many modern Greens. Its anti-industrialism may have been impractical, but it was translated through people like Howard and modern planners into suburbs and today's 'nimbyism'.

The success of these concepts—their practical expression rather than their utopian one, at least—stemmed from a number of things. First, Morris and his successors recognised the importance of becoming actively involved in the party-political process—in this case the emerging British Labour Party. Second, they articulated an intellectual vision which offered a decisive alternative to the industrialism that seemed to be destroying society. Third, they set out to convince opinion leaders of their arguments, in the belief that converting opinion leaders was the first step in converting the society as a whole.

In Australia, modern day environmentalism is epitomised by the continuing dispute over the extent and nature of logging of Australian eucalypts. Logging of native forests is generally agreed not to be Australia's biggest environmental problem—soil degradation, air pollution and waterways contamination are stronger candidates for that. Yet anyone looking at the environmental debate in Australia from outside could well think that trees were the central question.

While environmentalists in Australia started campaigning on a range of issues in the 1960s, in the 1970s they focused on forests. They adopted a number of techniques. First, asserting that forests were disappearing. This trend was, in fact, due to agriculture; forestry was actually enlarging our forested areas. Second, concentrating on particular harvesting practices even though they aid the natural regeneration process of eucalypts. Third, attacking the issue in small, well-defined geographic areas. The fight was never about forests as a whole, but always about a specific piece of forest which was always the 'last remnant' of some species or other.

This strategy was very successful largely because Australians rarely see their forests. We form are a highly urbanised culture, and we cluster around the coastline of a large island continent. Australia's economic strength is based on commodity production: wool, wheat, minerals and so on. Yet the majority of the population work in service industries.

Industry initially responded to the environmental campaigns by stressing the economic importance of forest products. That was next to useless, because there was no link in the public's mind between economic well-being and the distant forests. Indeed, the tide against the industry did not begin to ebb, even marginally, until the industry invested millions in advertising, education and public relations—efforts designed to inform people that the forests were not disappearing and that forestry practices were environmentally sound.

The history of environmental politics has important implications for the new millennium. It shows that you cannot fight against environmental campaigns simply on the basis of facts—you need to tap into the emotional elements of what it is that helps form people's opinions. It also indicates that passion about wilderness is in direct proportion to distance from the wilderness about which people are passionate. Both urbanisation and the distance between the ordinary lives of the population and the reality of production increase the attractiveness of wilderness. If the closest you ever get to a farm, a mine or a factory is a set of numbers on a computer screen, then arguments about jobs and industries are less effective than appeals to wilderness preservation are.

Most importantly, however, there is a strong correlation between rising standards of living and environmental awareness. The owners of the dark satanic mills moved away from the mills and the air pollution as soon as better transport made it possible for them to. Their workers wanted to do the same. In this respect, the environmental debate is over—we are never going to go back to the horrors of the past. As nations in Asia go through the same process they too will see the same correlation come to determine their environmental policies as rising living standards lead to increased demands for a better quality of life.

Successful environmental campaigns, while they use many modern communication techniques, still rely heavily on personal voluntary efforts over long periods by large numbers of people.

Those voluntary efforts and those large numbers of people are very often from Generation MM. Generation MM is not, therefore, going to retreat from environmentalism and associated demands that companies be environmentally responsible.

By the early 21st century most nations will be preparing national accounts which integrate both environmental and resource assets. Australia is already one of a number of countries committed to environmental accounting, as part of an international United Nations strategy on sustainable development. The accounts will be designed to look at the environmental implications of economic growth, at the contributions to environmental problems and at the implications of the use of regulation, taxation and incentives for environmental policy.

While the push is on for national environmental accounts, the pressure will also be on individual companies. A decade ago a few companies produced glossy environmental brochures. Today an increasing number are producing detailed reports which include data on environmental performance. By the new millennium many will be producing independently audited environmental reports side by side with their annual financial accounts. The companies that don't will be shunned by Generation MM as not reflecting the values of the new millennium.

Making demands on companies for greater environmental responsibility and more openness about environmental performance is easy. For an individual, in a consumer society, making changes is more difficult. And when the changes are driven by fear of an environmental apocalypse the complexities of resolving conflicts between beliefs and behaviours are immense. That's why people in the new millennium will fear an environmental apocalypse but will generally respond, not by transforming their lives but, as we will see, by recycling their household garbage!

To some, of course, the transformation is still the dream. That's why a Patriarch, an environmentalist and a philosopher got together to pursue a cause—a cause echoing the apocalyptic visions of Revelations.

The meeting, *The Economist* reported on 30 September 1995, marked the 1900th anniversary of the Book of Revelation and involved discussions between environmental activists and the leaders of the Orthodox Church.

Arranged by Patriarch Batholomew, the meeting explored the concept of the apocalypse and how religion and environmentalism could work together. The meeting was reportedly not hugely successful, but it did highlight the modern parallels between religious fundamentalism, apocalyptic thinking, millenarian hopes and environmentalism.

Predictions of environmental devastation are commonplace. Each year the Worldwatch Institute puts out a set of new predictions about mass starvation, energy crises and population overload. Despite the Club of Rome's predictions being demonstrated to be wide of the mark, environmentalists are constantly warning of some new apocalypse.

The problem for environmentalists is that the world's population is listening but not acting on the predictions. The problem for industry is that in resolving their dilemma the public can create new problems.

A *New Scientist* report of 2 December 1995, on research at Warwick University Business School, showed that 'greening is most successful where government incentives or regulations are involved'. Looking further into the report, it appears that 'green' products tend not to succeed unless they are given a regulatory advantage. Where there is a significant price difference or a major lifestyle trade-off, the consumer remains suspicious of green products. This is partly a reflection of the fact that consumers have a fairly well-developed sense of environmental awareness already. It is not that they are not wanting to do what they see as the right thing environmentally, but that they realise that many so-called green products are only marginally, if at all, environmentally superior to the alternatives. The real problem is that many environmentalists attach emotional and campaigning significance to green products and strive to increase their use. If they can't do this by persuasion they will follow the course they favour for all environmental problems—more regulation.

The public's dilemma is also illustrated by the Western world's continuing love affair with the car. The Australian Automobile Association, in a survey of motorists' priorities and attitudes, found that 80 per cent of motorists are concerned about the effects of cars on the environment but that only 20 per cent said they would reduce their use of cars. In November 1995 *New Scientist* reported that the University of Oxford's Transport Studies Unit had found that 60 per cent of United Kingdom car owners felt strongly that trying to reduce their car use would disrupt their family life and work. Even 30 per cent of non–car owners believed that the car was too convenient to give up 'for the sake of the environment'.

In essence, people are faced with a series of difficult trade-offs. They want to be environmentally responsible. They are concerned about the use of their cars and they worry about the impact of pollution.

Most people resolve the conflict by focusing on some symbolic environmental activity—in the Western world, either concern for the wilderness or household recycling, or both. Four million Australian households now have access to a kerbside recycling scheme—largely created by beverage container manufacturers and fillers through their industry association, the Litter Research and Recycling Association. Each week when households put out their bottles, cans and paper for the local council to pick up they are making their personal contribution to saving the world. It may not be massive, but it is seen by individuals as significant, and it certainly beats living in the wilderness without gas, electricity or water.

The way that individuals approach environmental issues suggests that one of the key challenges for businesses in the 21st century will be to ensure that they reassure people about environmental performance. This is not just a matter of offering warm-sounding hopes that everything will be all right. It is a matter of systematically communicating the point that the environment is improving. There is little doubt that air quality in London is now better and that it is possible to catch fish in the Thames. There are now more trees in the northeastern States of America than at any time since soon after European settlement. The Greening Australia program—operating through hundreds of local Landcare groups—is tackling the problems of soil degradation and erosion through tree plantings and other measures. This program is just a small part of the more than $5 billion spent each year in Australia on environment protection.

There is also the possibility that more people will begin to understand the immense regenerative power of nature. According to Claude Levi-Strauss, in his soon to be published book *Saudes do Brazil,* even the massive 'primeval' forests of Brazil, which have featured so much in international green campaigns, are a result of regeneration. He claims that aerial photographs demonstrate that, from about the first millennium BC, there were hundreds of thousands of hectares of the Amazon basin occupied by communities which had developed complex agricultural pursuits. He says that much of the 'primeval' forest in fact was 'reclaimed [by nature] after the Indians who had cleared and cultivated it were exterminated or pushed to the high ground between the valleys'.

In Australia, the lunar landscape left around Queenstown on the western coast of Tasmania by the Mt Lyell mining company was so bizarre that it became a tourist destination. In recent years the local council has come to be concerned about the future of the tourist potential, as nature begins to reclaim the area with grasses and shrubs.

There are many positive developments on the environment front. To offset the fears of Generation MM it will be imperative that business communicate these successes as well as responding to the sensations of the apocalyptic imagination.

I'm not going near the wilderness but I know how precious it is

An inevitable consequence of growing urbanisation is that people will have less and less contact with nature. The inevitable consequence of this is that their yearning for the natural will increase, while their capacity to fulfil the yearning is diminished.

Recognition of this phenomenon led to a campaign, late in the 19th century, to create a national parks service in the United States. In 1891 the United States Congress passed legislation which allowed the President to set aside areas of forest as national parks. Concurrently, nature writers such as John Muir were popularising the therapeutic, recreational role of wilderness areas. And, also concurrently, an exceptional politician emerged. Teddy Roosevelt came from a moderately wealthy family in New York City and was educated by private tutors, at Harvard and later at Columbia Law School. The epitome, one might say, of the Eastern establishment.

Yet Teddy was, in the public mind, not the epitome of the establishment but rather an explorer, adventurer, Rough Rider and rancher. Disraeli said of Gladstone's hobby—cutting down trees—that his pastimes were as destructive as his policies. And modern day environmentalists would be shocked by Roosevelt's portrayal of himself as an environmentalist. The animal liberationists who conducted the campaigns that ultimately led, among other things, to the Hudson's Bay company getting out of the fur business would certainly have targeted Teddy—the keen trophy hunter.

As President he did many things, but one of his most lasting achievements was the dramatic expansion of the area of 'national forest'. His predecessors had used the 1891 Forest Reserves Act to reserve some 16 million hectares. In just seven years—after Roosevelt had set the pace, broadened the legislation and campaigned for reservations—an additional 78 million hectares were reserved.

There are several points of significance in this. The United States was no longer a frontier society—it had become a great industrial power. Yet the power of the frontier myth was still enormous. Roosevelt seized on this paradox and put forward an idealistic vision of man and nature, as a way of meeting Americans' desire to recapture their heritage. He promoted this vision with a brilliant use of the new communications technology: news photography, early cinema, tabloid journalism. In doing so he created an image of himself which was as distant from his beginnings as America had become from its.

As Simon Schama's recent book *Landscape and Memory*[22] shows, people throughout history have projected on to landscape a vision about themselves and their society. The emergence of German identity, for instance, was closely linked to images of and legends about the vast northern European forests. With urbanisation accelerating, the chances of direct contact with landscape are correspondingly reduced. Moreover, the lifestyles of many modern people hardly prepare them for jaunts into the wilderness. Schama reproduces hundreds of drawings, paintings and book extracts that show how people reacted to all of this by approaching landscape and nature more and more through representations rather than through reality.

Today we have unparalleled opportunities to see such representations through the images that modern technology can provide from the most remote sites on the globe or in space. The more we are deprived of contact with nature the more we will search out these representations. And the more we see the representations, rather than the reality, the more precious the wilderness will be. The world will be changing constantly for Generation MM—but they will know that out there in some remote location there is a wilderness, pristine and untouched.

When Exxon's supertanker *Valdez* spilt a vast quantity of oil over such an untouched wilderness the outrage was immense. Most of those outraged had never visited the area. But they knew of it—and the damage done—through images that had made it precious. Exxon behaved throughout the incident as if they didn't share that view, didn't care about the spill, and that it was merely a technical problem to be solved by the engineers on the spot. The result—the outrage mounted instead of abating.

The lesson for every company in the new millennium is obvious: the wilderness is sacred and its violators will be punished by those who worship it.

I want to talk to *you*—not the modem!

People may yearn for family, aspire to the mystical, devoutly defend the environment and celebrate their important myths. But much of their lives will still take place in physical surroundings—homes, apartments, communities and offices.

The pace of technological change suggests that the physical environment will be some sort of technopolis. The need to protect an individual's identity and sense of belonging suggests that this technopolis—if it is to work for people—will need to provide for social interaction as well as communication by fibre optic cable.

Nothing illustrates this better than a model community, called Celebration, being built in Florida by the Disney Company. The community was originally a dream of the late Walt Disney, but was shelved while the company developed its various theme parks and continued its immensely successful entertainment business. Now the community is being developed. It will be the most modern, fully wired, technopolis in the world. Every new technology and communication device will be available within it. It is designed to use all of Silicon Valley's best products and services in order to create the community of the future.

But the community is going to be unusual in one other respect. It is going—externally—to resemble the small town United States communities which people associate with a glorious American past. There will be front porches, picket fences, town squares and all the ingredients necessary to ensure that the residents go back to the future rather than forward.

What is significant about the Disney Celebration community is that it rejects many of the commonly held assumptions about how technology will shape the future. The conventional view is that more and people will telecommute from their homes. Voting, shopping, banking, education and conversation will all take place through some interactive technology. In the office people will have 'hot desks' which they visit from time to time. Most of the time they will be on the road, tapping in by modem the material they have recorded in their handheld computer.

Charles Handy, London Business School fellow and successful business author, has speculated on the future of people in the virtual organisation. Writing in the May–June 1995 *Harvard Business Review,* he points out the number of organisations in which physical buildings are not necessary—using the highly successful Open University as a prime example. At the Open University there are thousands of students and many staff who join together through remote communication rather than in a physical classroom. But, Handy says, in such organisations a crucial determinant of success will be the trust between employee and employer. And he says, further, that to build that trust we need personal interaction: 'Paradoxically, the more virtual the organisation the more its people need to meet in person'. This will develop a sense of belonging and of community.

What the technological revolution cannot change is the fact that humans are sociable, gregarious animals. They want to interact with other humans and they do want to belong and have a sense of community.

Technology may make the isolation of telecommuting and the home office possible. It has made it easier to communicate with more people than ever before. But business people still get on planes to fly to meetings because there are moments when people must look each other in the eye, and get the reassurance of personal contact. And many office workers will want to decorate their working area with something personal and unique to them, in order to define it as *their* space.

The hopes of the proponents of 'hot desks' and the virtues of the virtual organisation will never change this reality. Indeed, in the new uncertainty of the new millennium—when belonging and security become even more important—the organisations that seek to diminish social interaction may merely diminish themselves.

3 Political and economic structures in the new millennium

I get intensely agitated when my garbage isn't collected by the local council. I get angry when the council fails to cut the lawns in the gardens opposite my house. But when Moody's shifts Australia's credit rating up or down a notch I simply note the news and wonder what impact it will have on the thinking of the business community.

The relative intensity of my responses is a reflection of the realities of my power. If the council doesn't collect the garbage I can ring up its general manager and make their life so miserable that it's easier for them to provide the service I need. If Moody's changes its rating I can deal with the consequences as far as its impact on business perceptions is concerned—but beyond that I can do little about the decision.

In the new millennium this contrast is going to be more and more vividly apparent to Generation MM. As a result, Generation MM will learn to live with new approaches to international, national and local politics. It will seek involvement where that involvement can make a difference—at the local level. Simultaneously, in areas where Generation MM people suspect that involvement cannot make a difference—at the national level—the political players will be forced to try harder to arrest their attention, with new policies, new symbols and new promises seeking to get them involved enough to at least vote. And where it definitely can't make a difference—at the global level—

Generation MM will respond, in reacting against its powerlessness, by embracing philosophies and ideologies different from those of the current conventional wisdom.

Today, business, the media and the politicians in Anglo-Saxon countries all subscribe to a broad *laissez faire* capitalist ideology. Under this ideology the market can do no wrong and can solve all problems. As we will see, Generation MM will almost certainly not share the same view.

Where do I belong?

There was one thing the markets and the Marxists always agreed on: the nation state was an obstacle in the path of the evolution of a truly global world, united and co-operative.

Looking back over the past few centuries—particularly our own—it seems as if nationalism has been a force for evil more than anything else. The first European nation states were the Netherlands, France, Sweden, England, Spain and Portugal. From the 16th century to the 18th century they spent much of their time at war with each other or planning to be at war with each other, or in alliance with various combinations of each other. In the 19th century a host of new nations—for example Germany and Italy—appeared, while other states, like Poland, were united and dismembered at various times. In the 20th century nationalism lurched over into aggressive chauvinism, with the devastating result of two world wars. Since those wars nationalism has been the impetus for a variety of colonial and other wars in Africa and Asia.

In some accounts of his historical development these events have been knitted into a story in which, progressively, nation states emerge and then evolve into a new global society which will dominate the world during the 21st century. But what is becoming clear is that in the 21st century the nation state will not only continue to be important—but that within it progressively smaller and smaller communities will come to be highly significant.

A symbol of this new thinking is the sudden resurgence of interest in Johann Gottfried Herder—the 18th century German philosopher considered to be the founder of cultural nationalism. In the period immediately after World War II Herder dropped into a sort of oblivion, seemingly blamed along with other nationalist philosophers for the horrendous crimes committed in the name of nationalism in the middle of the 20th century. The break up of the Russian empire and the re-emergence of the Baltic and other states as independent nations appeared to be the catalyst for the renewed interest in Herder. National cultures and the nations they represented were becoming important again.

A number of other philosophers also began to look anew at the question of nationalism. Charles Taylor, a Canadian who had thought deeply about Canadian identity and the Canadian Constitution, is probably the best known of them. But his view of nationalism—shaped perhaps by his Canadian origins—is different from the more traditional views. He is wary of the 'evils' of nationalism, while stressing the importance of shared values and common identities for a harmonious society. Yet he still argues that 'deep diversity is the only formula on which a united federal Canada can be rebuilt'.

We are even seeing new statelets and new ethnic groupings emerging—sometimes helped into being more by the study of perceptions of ethnicity than by rediscovering history. Writing in the *Times Literary Supplement* of 17 November 1995, the editor Ferdinand Mount reviewed two new books on nationalism. In passing, he mentioned that a Professor of Ukrainian Studies in Toronto was promoting a 'Lemko national revival' in present day Poland. The 'revival' involved a small cluster of East Slavs who don't, until recently, appear to have thought of themselves as a nation at all. In another case a German scholar has devised a new alphabet and a new 'nationalism' for a small group of people who speak a language related to Georgian.

But despite such examples the overall trend is significant. History is being revisited in older nation states. Basque separatism has moved from being a terrorist movement to a force to be reckoned with at national level in Spain. The Lombard League in Italy reactivates a separatist past which is only a hundred years old. As Ferdinand Mount points out, 'the present boundaries of the United Kingdom are less than 80 years old' and the United Kingdom itself is less than 300 years old. The Canadian dilemma over Quebec and the North American Free Trade Agreement has got as much to do with ancient events—the 1849 Annexation Manifesto, the 1783 loyalist emigration to Canada, the fall of Quebec and the fact that Canada is one of only two nations to have defeated the United States in a war since 1776—as it does with contemporary events.The ugly side of nationalism is also still apparent, with extreme right-wing and anti-immigrant groups emerging in the United Kingdom, France, Germany and Austria over recent years.

But the resurgence of interest in nationalism today seems to be qualitatively different from that of the past. First, no nation—as the French discovered after Mitterand was first elected—can run an independent economic policy. Second, when economic nationalism is impossible because of the globalisation of markets it is cultural nationalism that becomes more significant. And cultural nationalism is about the diversity of themes, peoples and interests within a community. When the United Kingdom is concerned about its sovereignty within the European Union it is really asserting English cultural nationalism. Many in Scotland and Wales see the EU as a framework within which they can reassert their cultural nationalism against the domination of British nationalism. Indeed, the very notion of subsidiarity—that authority within a structure should reside at the lowest levels possible (which the United Kingdom uses as an argument against EU supranationalism)—is an argument against the existence of the United Kingdom itself! Even in the United States—One Nation Under God since Lincoln and the Civil War—the individual States have identities which are both different and jealously protected.

The step from old-style nationalism to cultural nationalism has important implications for government. The chief characteristics of the old nation state were strong central government and a strong state. Yet in the new millennium the once strong state will be weak in the face of global markets, their whims and movements.

Ironically, while it was common to see belief in the nation—and in cultural nationalism—as emotional and irrational, the markets were seen as cool, rational and ruthless. Generation MM, however, may well come to believe that it is cultural nationalism which is rational and international markets which are irrational.

Who do you call first—your stockbroker or your psychologist?

Each day about $1 trillion is traded on foreign exchange markets. The movement of funds can destabilise governments, send currencies plummeting and destroy economic plans. These markets are elevated by governments, the media and themselves to mystical status, and economic policies are evaluated in terms of whether the markets will find them acceptable or not. But the markets are not just some mystical 'invisible hand'. They are actually made up of people. The Europeans call the markets the 'Anglo-Saxon' markets because the people who work in them are mostly American or English. Most of them are young and, while they no longer all wear red braces and striped shirts, they do share a common outlook on life. That outlook is not, however, always informed by detailed knowledge of the places and markets in which they invest. Richard Mayne, former personal assistant to Jean Monnet—one of the architects of the European Commission—wrote in the *Times Literary Supplement* of 12 January 1996 that currency speculators are easily spooked.

He recounted three episodes to illustrate this. In one case, the markets sold the Irish pound after they misunderstood a local idiom, 'not today or tomorrow', which was used in response to a question about exchange rate movements. The phrase is meant to convey 'never', but the bright boys and girls in the markets thought it probably meant some time after the day after tomorrow. The second Mayne example: when the simple act of calling a media conference without actually saying what it was about triggered speculation on the Danish krone: The third: when dealers misread an interest rate rise and the Spanish peseta plummeted. There are many other examples. As cynics remarked after the Mexican and other emerging economies' disasters of 1995, some of the market operators had only just begun to find out where the countries they were investing in were, when they had to pull out again!

Another problem in predicting and understanding markets is the impact of chaos. *The Economist* reported on 13 January 1996 that chaos was 'under a cloud' because financial markets had been hoping to use chaos theory as a means of projecting market movements. *The Economist*, of course, didn't think the theory was under a cloud. What had happened was that because financial markets behave chaotically (in the mathematical sense), chaos theory was believed to be a key which might unlock the market's mysteries. In fact, because of the nature of the theory itself, and our inability to understand all the factors which influence markets, the attempt was doomed to failure.

On the other hand, while markets may be chaotic, at times they show—like other chaotic systems—patterns of movement. Theoretically, if we can understand the patterns we can make a great amount of money. In the past decade serious computing power and serious mathematical minds have been put to work in the hope that the secret of how to make serious money might be cracked. So far it hasn't been, mainly because of another fundamental law of economics and finance: indicators cease to be useful as tools as soon as people start to use them. If people discover a previously unknown pattern or relationship, the minute it becomes known it loses its effect.

A further problem is that many of the 'patterns' are probably just coincidences exposed by the might of the computer power applied. *The Economist* of 2 September 1995 reported on a new study by Jeremy Siegel, Professor of Finance at the Wharton School, University of Pennsylvania. Among Siegel's findings were these: around the world, share prices tend to fall in September; small firms' shares tend to do well in January; and shares tend to fall on Monday and to rise on the final trading day of each month. In 1993 a researcher found that shares tend to do worse on cloudy days. There may well be rational explanations for all these phenomena or they may just be chance patterns. Whichever, they will disappear when the markets factor them into their calculations.

The fabulously successful international currency speculator, George Soros, ought to be given the last word on the markets which have made him a billionaire. In his recent book *Soros on Soros*,[23] he says: 'Where I am at odds with the latter-day apostles of laissez faire is that I don't believe markets are perfect. In my opinion they are just as likely to lead to unsustainable excesses as to equilibrium'.

It could be that the most rational explanation of how markets move has to do with the mood swings and prejudices of the traders. One of the most important and persistent characteristics of markets appears to be that they frequently exhibit 'herd behaviour'. This form of behaviour is the major explanation for the periodic bursts of insanity—the long ago South Sea Bubble, the 1987 crash and the next market crash, whenever that might be—that affect markets. What is remarkable is that all such episodes tend to have common themes—particularly greed, stupidity and repentance, followed by another boom a little later on—which have psychological rather than economic explanations.

So, if herd behaviour is the explanation, in the new millennium perhaps we should be studying mob psychology rather than mathematics if we want to unravel the mysteries of the markets. And we should be wondering whether the mob is now more a characteristic of markets than it is of the nationalism that plagued the 20th century.

It is also herd behaviour that explains why—with both markets and politics—the conventional wisdom is often wrong.

. . . And *is* the conventional wisdom often wrong?

The economist J. K. Galbraith has made many contributions in many different areas: economics, politics and education. But his insight—that the conventional wisdom is—as he put it not just often but 'always' wrong—has a special piquancy in a millennium age.

The insight is a very sound, but not infallible, basis for understanding what goes on in the world and what's about to happen next. It's useful as a way of understanding horseracing, politics, economics, share price movements and similar things. It works like this. When everyone you know—colleagues, all the media, all the politicians, everyone in the public relations and advertising industry, all the markets—are telling you that the current conventional wisdom is the latest, best and most enduring concept of all time, that is exactly the moment to jump off the bandwagon. The idea has just had its day!

An old variation on the theme was the adage that the time to start selling shares was when the lift driver gave you stockmarket tips. There are very few lift drivers left these days, so it's hard to test the theory. Moreover, my mother, who drove a lift for many years, also distrusted the idea, because she worked in a bank and she wasn't sure—on the basis of what she heard of the managers' lending policies—that the lift drivers weren't in fact a lot smarter than the managers were.

Now, despite Galbraith's insight, it is obvious that stubborn contrarian investment policies can be disastrous. Short selling, just because a boom has started, is a quick way to go bankrupt. Following a boom can make you wealthy. But the broader notion of straw hats in winter and umbrellas in summer is a good guide to how a contrarian approach—based on the notion that the conventional wisdom is always wrong—can work.

It works because the Galbraith insight illustrates that there are longer term cycles of opinion at work shaping society. In the 20th century we have focused very strongly on the short term—the moment at which the conventional wisdom appears right. But the business cycle has not been abolished and the Kondratieff theories, which suggest that longer term 40 to 50 year economic cycles exist, are still looking remarkably robust when you examine the historical record. These longer term cycles often occur over about a generation and reflect changes in attitudes between generations. For instance, assuming that Generation MM will share the conventional wisdom of the 1980s and early 90s is a recipe for proving Galbraith right.

A few examples illustrate how social and political opinion is formed over long periods. It is arguable that the key long-term factors shaping French society were the clerical and anti-clerical disputes which came to a head in the Dreyfus affair in the 1890s. The Dreyfus affair, in which a Jewish officer of the French army was falsely accused of spying for Germany, provoked bitter divisions within French society. The fundamental divisions dated back a century and more to the debates of the Enlightenment period and were between the old-style monarchist Catholic conservatives (the clericals) and the new republican and radical forces (the anti-clericals). For the next 70 years or so the fight continued. Even in the 1980s the then French Minister for Culture, Jack Lang, faced protests when he wanted to erect a statue of Dreyfus in the Tuileries. One event—the Dreyfus affair—was a catalyst that shaped debate over several generations.

The changing attitudes to the economics of Lord Keynes are another example. Around 1930, when Keynes first articulated his ideas, he was regarded as a dangerous radical who would end the era of sound money. Those who have read his work will realise that he was many things but dangerous radical was not one of them. A deeply conservative economist, he was committed to improving the functioning of capitalism by trying to protect it from the booms, busts and depressions which undermined its appeal. By 1945, when the Keynesian consensus ruled, anyone who disagreed with Keynes was considered a dangerous radical. In the early 1970s President Nixon said—just as the Keynesian consensus was disintegrating—'we are all Keynesians now'. And by 1985 anyone who cited Keynes was regarded as foolish and as failing to recognise the realities of the new free market consensus.

The patterns behind such long-term changes seem to emerge in the following way. First a few intellectuals start to work away in a particular discipline. They start to gain attention and publicity. (These days they form a thinktank.) Then the ideas get swept up into the mainstream and sweep across the world. Politicians speak of them with authority and the ideas become the ruling conventional wisdom. At that point some other intellectuals start questioning this new conventional wisdom and begin beavering away until they overturn it and erect a new paradigm.

In the short term, chaos and the contrarian approaches explain why economists get it so wrong when it comes to forecasting. In the longer term, the cycles by which public attitudes are formed explain how the conventional wisdom is changed from generation to generation.

The wheel is turning now. In the new millennium Generation MM is almost certainly going to subscribe to a conventional wisdom different from today's. The odds are that it will be a rejection of much of today's wisdom. But then it will only be a few decades before yet another 21st century generation works to overturn the Generation MM conventional wisdom. Later—in chapters on corporate cultures, marketing and corporate structures—we look at how business can ensure that it has read the cycle correctly.

Quick, wave the flag—and hope no one notices what's really going on

In a global economy the actions of individual governments are becoming less and less relevant and, as governments have decreasing impact on economic reality, they are turning more and more to symbols—and to social policy—to position themselves as different from their political opponents. At the same time they are using hyperbole to heighten the significance of what they say and do, and issues of no real international significance are debated with intense heat and as ferociously as if the future of the universe were at stake.

In Australia the Victorian Premier calls people who disagree with his policies 'traitors'. The previous Australian Prime Minister called his opponents 'scum'. In the United States, right-wingers openly advocate the overthrow of the government and canvass the possibility of the President being assassinated. Generosity of spirit, tolerance and liberalism seem to have disappeared from political discourse. All politicians are convinced they are right. The people in power are, according to the opposition, always the worst and most disastrous government yet. They can do no right. The people in opposition, according to the government, would wreck the paradise the government has created and set the nation back years.

The notion of an intellectual marketplace, with *ideas* competing, disappears under the onslaught of conviction politics.

Most of the intensity, of course, is about matters that are really more symbol than reality. Among the big issues of the past few years in the United States were: whether the President had inhaled drugs and whether he had had sex with women other than his wife; gays in the military; abortion; and whether there should be a constitutional amendment to ban flag burning. The serious Budget impasses between Congress and the President got sidetracked by a contretemps about whether or not the House Speaker, on a Presidential flight, had been made to sit at the back of the plane. In Australia, the issues have been the flag and the republic. In the United Kingdom, law and order, the Royal Family and sleaze have attracted more column inches and television footage than almost any other issue.

The President's character is a symbol of debate about family values; the flag-burning issue about patriotism; the Royal Family and law and order about traditional visions of British society and social class and the new realities of second class global status. This symbolic focus is a product of the fact that national governments are less powerful than ever before and less and less capable of making changes to the state they govern.

The classic example is the contrast between Italy and the United Kingdom. By late 1995 the Italians had had 55 governments since World War II. Taxes haven't been efficiently collected. Corruption has been endemic. Administration has been lax to non-existent. Yet in that period Italy has come back from being a defeated power to become one of the biggest and most successful economies in the world—surpassing the United Kingdom in economic output in the process.

The Italian case has admittedly been special. Its centuries-long history of innovative communities—highlighted in his work on competitive advantage by Professor Michael Porter[24]—has allowed industries such as clothing and textiles to flourish in Italy, when in most of the rest of the developed world they have succumbed to competition from low wage countries. But, special or not, one has to ask questions about the Italian experience. Newspapers and political leaders are always talking about the need for government to provide strong direction. No political speech goes by without the words 'firm', 'decisive' and so on being trotted out. While Italy was surpassing the United Kingdom economically, Britain had one of its strongest governments of the 20th century. One cannot but help ask whether anarchy is preferable to leadership.

The emphasis on symbols and leadership is, of course, no accident. Deep in their souls—despite the television interviews, the chauffeured limousines and the deference accorded them—most modern political leaders comprehend the limits of their power. They know that the attitude they strike is more significant than the policy they develop. They know that, even if they do develop a detailed and coherent policy, it will get no more media coverage than a bright barb against their opponent will.

But there is an alternative to their powerlessness—a resort to symbolism and to social policy. Attitudes to gender, environmental regulation, sport, culture and so on can be used to differentiate political parties and to create an image of power and decisiveness.

But Generation MM will realise that things are changing.

As globalism diminishes the power of national governments, the relevance of the strong central state diminishes as well. Why shouldn't a region, a community or whatever have more say about the things that matter to it. And the things that matter are garbage collection, planning laws, parks, local museums and local culture—the areas in which government can still have an impact on the daily, immediate lives of people.

A Moody's rating does have an effect on individuals—but the effect is attenuated and indirect. The effectiveness of a garbage collection contract, in contrast, is a direct determinant of the quality of a person's life.

In the 21st century Generation MM will ask loudly why real power can't be devolved, as they strive to wrest power away from the Whitehalls, the Washingtons, the Bonns and the Canberras—and give it back to the local community.

Be careful—the pinks are back under the bed

The growing awareness of the irrationality of markets, the increasing emphasis on cultural nationalism and the desire to give power back to local areas are going to have profound implications for the current conventional wisdom on 'economic rationalism'. Indeed, in the new millennium it is highly probable that the era of 'economic rationalism' will be replaced by an emphasis on new forms of social democracy.

If there was one word that dominated 1980s economic and political debate it was 'market'. If there is one word that will dominate economic and political debate in the early 21st century it is 'community'.

In the period immediately after 1945 the Keynesian consensus on full employment, government intervention and the mixed economy was basically accepted by all the major Western political parties. In the 1980s this postwar consensus unravelled and a new consensus on the role of markets, deregulation and privatisation emerged. In 1945 the Keynesian consensus was the conventional wisdom and only very few people—Hayek and others—challenged it. Today, the new market consensus is the conventional wisdom and very few people are challenging it. Just as nobody thought in 1945 that the consensus would ever change, so today everyone is convinced that the ruling ideas will go on forever.

Yet during the 1980s and early 1990s there were already some trends emerging to suggest that a change might be closer than people think. The change will not be revolutionary—communism is not about to come back. But then the change in the countries that embraced the new market consensus was hardly revolutionary either. For example, despite the rhetoric of the Conservative Government, public spending in Britain still accounts for more than 40 per cent of GDP—just as high as it was when the Conservatives came to power in 1979.

The change will be more a matter of emphasis—a change between what Anglo-Saxon countries call 'the market' and what Europeans call the 'social market'. What the Europeans mean by this term is that the market is the basic underpinning of the system but that in some areas—particularly social policy—it doesn't deliver satisfactory results. The community needs at times to step in and fix problems. The most visible differences between the two systems are the absence from western European cities of the abject poverty and inner city devastation seen in United States cities, and the attractive and efficient infrastructure—trains, roads and public facilities—in Europe.

The key trend pointing in this new direction is the rejection of materialism. The 1980s were an era when greed was good and where individual interest was paramount. The system was meant to favour the individual over the state. In fact the argument was never that simple. European philosophers had been discussing the balance between social and individual interests for a century and more. The 19th century thinkers

Wilhelm Heinrich Riehl and Karl Tonnies evolved two concepts which defined the differences between various societies. One concept was called *gemeinschaft*—a term used to describe an organically bonded community. The other was called *gesellschaft*—an aggregate of individuals connected only by material interests. Various Anglo-Saxon thinkers—Thoreau in America; Ruskin and Carlyle in Britain—took up the debate and applied the concepts to the societies in which they lived. Tonnies, incidentally, moved on to a more mystical approach, in which he claimed that the important influences on society were forests and wilderness and their impact on folk memory and nationalism—another trend that has become extremely significant.

The most obvious example of the debate's relevance today is the state of most Western conservative parties. These parties are a curious amalgam of *gemeinschaft* and *gesellschaft*. On the one hand, they are traditional conservatives in favour of the family, of good, of authority and tradition. On the other hand, they favour free markets and all the libertarian ideas that these bring. The fact is that capitalism has been the most powerful revolutionary force in history—that's why it has been so successful. It changes things and changes them often. It doesn't stand still and it doesn't respect tradition. This is why many old-fashioned conservatives opposed the free market push of the 1980s—because they saw the threat it posed to traditional conservative values—and are now questioning the future of economic rationalism. A prominent Australian Catholic intellectual, B. A. Santamaria, has always been seen as a conservative and a supporter of conservative political parties. Yet today, in his writings, he is echoing the views of Karl Marx's colleague, Engels, in asserting that the problem with free market capitalism is that it reduces everything to the status of a cash commodity.

Throughout the world similar conservative intellectuals are raising similar questions. In the United States the debate is even more complicated by debate about rights. The problem with arguments about the pre-eminence of the rights of individuals is that they run smack bang into the problem that individuals have obligations too. The whole aim of society is to balance the two. Arguably, the failure to reconcile the two is responsible for the emergence of a 'victim' society in America. In the victim society everybody is entitled to do almost anything they like. No one is ever at fault for whatever they do because it is the result of their being black, white, female, male, Hispanic, short, disabled, fat—or whatever. Victims arrogate to themselves rights by the law book pile, but never seem to accept that obligations exist as well.

At the same time as the traditional conservatives are raising questions, the young—Generation MM—are asking their own questions about values. The result—we have the ironic situation in which old-style social democrats, conservatives and the young are united by an idealistic, anti-materialist set of values opposed to the ruling 'economic rationalist' philosophy.

While all this has been happening a number of intellectuals have been beavering away in an attempt to undermine the new consensus—just as the old was undermined. Most of these people have been focusing on the notion of community, although others have been seeking to apply mainstream religious ideas to politics.

The most prominent of the first group of people is Amitaai Etzioni, who has written a book called *The Spirit of Community.*[25] Etzioni argues that community values—co-operation and consensus—are more important and more valuable than the materialist values of the market. His book has already been enormously influential in Britain and elsewhere in Europe and has been used as the basis for arguing that we must rebuild communities in order to rebuild values. Rebuilding communities means investing in infrastructure, ensuring that local government works effectively and—most importantly—re-establishing the importance of obligations in creating an organically bonded nation. And it could well also mean a resurgence of interest in community ownership of infrastructure, with a resulting decline in the speed and scope of privatisation.

The most famous example of the second group is Tony Blair, leader of the British Labour Party. Blair is no revolutionary; but he is in fact a radical. He is a devout Christian who has much in common with Christian social democrats across Europe. He wants, he says, to build a 'stakeholder economy'. Speaking in Singapore on 8 January 1996 he said:

> The economics of the centre and the centre-left today should be geared to the creation of the stakeholder economy which involves all our people, not a privileged few, or even a better-off 30 per cent or 40 per cent or 50 per cent. If we fail in that, we waste talent, squander potential wealth-creating ability and deny the basis of trust upon which a cohesive society, one nation, is built.

If we look at the words we see all the Generation MM values—trust, cohesion, stakeholding—that will shape the 21st century.

It was a very important speech and to some it seemed odd that it was given in Singapore. There were, of course, two reasons. First, Singapore is a good example of a stakeholder economy in which the government works hard to create a community consensus in which all individuals participate as stakeholders—through the highly successful superannuation system, for instance—in the city state's economic growth. Second, Blair was returning from a holiday in Australia—a holiday shared with a close friend, an Anglican priest from Oxford, who now lives in Australia. It has been said that British Labour always owed more to Methodism than to Marx. The aphorism reflects the extent to which religious values (particularly Christian concepts of equality and compassion) rather than concepts of class war impacted on British Labour policy. Blair is an Anglican, not a Methodist, but the sentiment still conveys a reality which will be relevant not only to Britain but to the rest of the world in the new millennium.

Eat Chinese, speak many tongues and respect Queen Victoria

These changes in attitudes to markets, nations and ideologies are inevitably going to be further influenced by changing economic and political power balances in the world. Predicting the nature of the changes seems simple. A quick survey of futurologists, political leaders and newspaper commentators on the identity of the next superpower would almost certainly find that either China or that entity known as the Asia–Pacific is the most popular candidate.

The European world, for much of the past five centuries, has always been dominated by one superpower or other. First Spain, briefly Holland, then France, then Britain and then the United States. This European dominance was interpreted as global dominance. Now—with the economic revolution in China and the astonishing economic growth in the region—we seem to have reached a point where a new superpower, or superpower grouping, is emerging. Some commentators, looking at the cancer eating at America's cities and its political life, even wonder whether the United States might implode in much the same way as the Russian state did, leaving the way clear for the 21st century to become the Asian era much more rapidly than many currently anticipate.

There is much to recommend this vision. On sheer growth rates alone, China and the rest of Asia—including Japan—should be the economic powerhouse of the 21st century.

Yet the vision actually obscures more than it hides. For a start, it is a very Eurocentric view of the world. China has always been a superpower—it just hasn't always decided to be part of the rest of the world. The sheer number of people in Asia and the history of its various societies—India, Vietnam, Japan, China and others—have meant that for most of human history Asia, Africa and the Middle East have been immensely important to the world. Felipe Fernandez Armesto, writing in the September 1995 magazine *History Today* about how this millennium might be seen in the next, imagined a new millennium Galactic Museum. In it the museum guide would look back on the 20th century and say:

> Towards the end of the second millennium Christian era, historians on Earth seem to have been unable to understand what was happening around them. Dazzled by their belief in the Rise of the West they were unaware that their planet was

reverting to type. They mistook the short-term trends of the 19th century for the overall character of the millennium.

The vision of a coming Asian century is also made seductive by the debate about Asian values and whether these have been decisive in encouraging the rapid growth of the 'tiger' economies of Asia. Singapore's Lee Kuan Yew has argued that the Confucian values of respect for elders, study, hard work, honesty, decency, responsibility and willingness to sacrifice individual interests for the good of the community have contributed to Asian success and Western decay. The Australian Department of Foreign Affairs and Trade commissioned a study from its East Asia Analytical Unit on overseas Chinese business networks in Asia in order to better understand the phenomenon. Two other Australians, Warren Reed and Reg Little, have written a book, *The Confucian Renaissance*,[26] arguing that the economic boom across East Asia rested on cultural similarities throughout the region.

In recent years, though, this Asiacentric vision of the future has come under attack. The main impetus for questioning the link between Asian values and the economic miracle came from Paul Krugman, a Stanford University economics professor who published an influential article, 'The Myth of Asia's Miracle', in *Foreign Affairs* in November 1994. Krugman argues that total factor productivity increases suggest that the Asian miracle is not quite as miraculous as is imagined. He says that much of the Asian miracle is a creation of Western myth-making. He also says that the West needs a competitor—in the 1950s it was Russia—to define itself against, and that Asia is fulfilling that role today.

That the Asian miracle is exportable, and not unique, is also clear. Massachusetts Institute of Technology researchers have studied the international automotive industry over many years. They published their findings in a book, *The Machine that Changed the World*,[27] which demonstrated that Japanese workplace techniques could readily be used anywhere else. The Japanese went to low wage areas of the United Kingdom that had poorly educated and poorly managed workers and trained them to achieve just as much as Japanese workers could. They did the same with computers and technology in Silicon Glen in Scotland.

And, after all, Confucian values—as listed above—sound remarkably like the Victorian values which built the British empire in the 19th century, rather than some new unique concept about to revolutionise the world.

A more profound problem in seeking to predict the most probable 21st century superpower is the assumption that there must be such a power. For the foreseeable future the United States and Russia are going to continue to be extraordinarily powerful, simply because both have the capacity to destroy the rest of the world with nuclear weapons. But sheer military might is not enough to shape the values and attitudes of the rest of the world. Russia has sunk into a gangster capitalism so bad that it makes the former Communists attractive to voters and is now unlikely to be a model for anyone. The United States, on the other hand, is the most influential country in the world, not because of its military power but because of the reach of its culture through the global dissemination of its manufactured products and its television, films and records.

The most likely outcome for the 21st century is that no one country or one culture will dominate—rather the dominant culture will be a fusion of many cultures.

The common language of this culture could well be English. According to the *New Scientist* of 6 January 1996, five languages—Chinese, English, Spanish, Russian and Hindi—are spoken by half the world already. Another 100 languages take the global language coverage up to 95 per cent. The thousands of smaller languages may well survive as part of the reviving emphasis on separatist culture, but it seems likely that the trend to a few dominant global languages will continue.

The new culture's values will probably be what we call Asian values—Victorian, if you are English—and the arts and wider culture will have many influences. Co-productions in film and television already occur across the globe. Chinese musicians play Western 19th century Romantic chamber music. Americans make kung fu movies. The Victorian State Opera trains singers from China. Japanese companies buy paintings by Impressionist artists who themselves were influenced by

Asian art. The United States, Europe and Australia are all becoming multicultural countries where diversity is the norm. They are becoming nations in which cultures have fused to create a new multifaceted culture. Asia itself is many countries, many peoples, many cultures, rather than one homogeneous geographic area. In the 1960s we spoke of Transatlantic Man to describe those people who seemed to live between Europe and America. I have a Japanese colleague, Shuji Hirose, who personifies the 21st century version of Transatlantic Man. He is equally at home in Hawaii, Hokkaido or Houston. Fluent in English and Japanese, he stands astride the Pacific—creating a new class for a new century—the Transpacific Person.

For the new millennium Shuji Hirose symbolises the magnificent global melting pot—driven by communications and travel—that is beginning to take shape. Communities will treasure their own traditions and cultures while being exposed to more and more of the culture of others. They will be proud of their regional cuisine and music while being equally able to enjoy the music and food of others.

In this new era Generation MM will be inclusive—not exclusive—and the dominant culture will be a hybrid in which diverse communities can prosper and survive.

Side by side with cultural nationalism, global markets and powerful local community groups will be a world population eating the cuisines of many nations, speaking many languages and espousing traditional values—all the time powerfully asserting their distinctiveness and their membership of their family community, region and nation.

4 The knowledge economy

One of the world's leading conductors, Claudio Abbado, took legal action in March 1996 against a record company—Deutsche Gramophon. He claimed that the company had released, without permission, a compilation of slow movements from his Mahler symphony performances and that this had compromised the integrity of the performances.

Almost simultaneously in Australia there was public outcry about the cost of CDs and the fact that they were twice as expensive as in other countries. Some disgruntled consumers began to buy their music through the Internet—by downloading performances from the Net.

The compilation of classic performances into mass-marketed CDs and tapes is common. The anarchic use of the Internet is equally common. However, both cases raise important new questions about the significance of knowledge to the world—about moral rights, copyright, contractual arrangements and the ultimate ownership of knowledge, art and artistic rights.

In the new millennium these questions will be typical of the complex issues that the new knowledge-based industries create. And, as we see shortly, the questions also suggest why the most successful Generation MM lawyer is likely to specialise in intellectual property rights rather than physical property rights.

Knowledge will be the most valuable commodity in the world

For centuries authors and thinkers have been writing about the link between knowledge and power. The scientific pioneer and legal official Francis Bacon coined the expression: 'knowledge itself is power'. Succeeding thinkers liked it so much that they used it again and again in various forms. The philosopher Thomas Hobbes shortened it to the form in which we know it best: 'knowledge is power'. The lexicographer Samuel Johnson developed the thought further and claimed that 'knowledge is more than equivalent to force'. The pre-eminent political cynic of the 19th century—British Prime Minister, Benjamin Disraeli—drawled that 'as a general rule the most successful man in life is the man who has the best information'.

In modern business thinking Peter Drucker has been the principal advocate of the Bacon thesis, saying: 'Today knowledge has power. It controls access to opportunity and advancement'.

For years business leaders and conservative politicians have exhorted their nations to work harder—or fall behind their competitors. But as the Australian political figure and author Barry Jones remarked in the 1970s, twenty men working harder and harder with picks and shovels still won't dig a ditch as fast as one with a bulldozer. As this reality became obvious, the new version of the exhortation was 'work smarter'. But even this was really just about doing things better and more efficiently. It was not really an advance on the Taylorist theories of the 1930s.

It is clear, however, that not only today but also to come in the 21st century we are dealing with a major shift in the significance and role of knowledge in the economy.

Writing in the *Australian Business Review Weekly* of 13 August 1995, David James summarised the thinking about knowledge of a variety of leading present day management writers and practitioners. Peter Drucker says:

> Knowledge is the only meaningful resource today. The traditional factors of production—land [natural resources], labour and capital—have not disappeared. But they have become secondary. Knowledge is now being applied systematically and purposefully to [the question of] what new knowledge is needed, whether it is feasible and what has to be done to make knowledge effective.

Tom Peters, that extraordinarily provocative and innovative writer and lecturer, says the new approach is about 'more intellect, fewer materials'. English management writer Charles Handy talks of the need to recognise that creativity and knowledge, rather than musclepower, add value—'Fewer people thinking better'.

In the quest for knowledge the Myer Foundation in Australia is supporting the Cranlana program—a non-profit scheme which encourages business and community leaders to tackle serious intellectual and philosophical questions. In a centre in one of Melbourne's leading residential suburbs, community and business leaders gather for weeklong discussions of the work of the great economic, political and philosophical thinkers in the Western world's history.

But what does all this enthusiasm for knowledge mean?

Proponents of the knowledge revolution are saying that the developed world has moved into a postindustrial economy. We are applying the intelligence and innovation we once applied to physical systems to information management. At its most basic level we are using knowledge to do things better.

At another level, however, we are actually creating new industries, new services and new ways of doing business. The remarkable thing about the millennial age is that it is almost impossible to know exactly down what paths the new knowledge-based economy will take us. We can see some of the outlines through the convergence of computing and communications, but the wonderful thing about knowledge is that it can lead us on—systematically or through serendipity—to totally new concepts.

So to prepare ourselves for the 21st century we should not be wasting our time puzzling about exactly what knowledge will be required and how it can be applied. Rather we need to focus on how we acquire knowledge and how we develop continuous learning systems.

The most effective knowledge acquisition system is simple. It involves three skills: the capacity to research information; the capacity to critically evaluate that information; and the capacity to synthesise it. With those skills we can approach any new area of activity, knowing how to acquire the information required to understand it. It is because of this that these three skills ought to be the basis of our education system.

But in a knowledge economy we need more than just the capacity to acquire and synthesise information. We also need to know how to use it creatively and effectively. Taking that step requires new, different and higher level skills. Providing the creativity is probably easier than we think. Because the vast majority of people down the centuries have been poorly educated, we have always tended to see the elite as especially creative.

Of course, the elite of the elite—the Beethovens, Picassos and so on—are creative to a degree that no amount of additional education will replicate. But creativity of a lesser order is within the reach of most well-educated people—simply because of the nature of our brain circuitry. It is easy to forget that the brain is the most sophisticated computer in the world. It is capable of feats of memory, calculation and synthesis that are astounding. In particular, it has a remarkable capacity to make connections. Creativity—at less than the super-elite level—is really about these connections. How often do you hear people say that some individual has bright ideas? Normally, the reality is that that person has acquired information, then their brain links the information with something—makes the connection—and allows a bright idea to pop out.

If this is the reality behind creativity then we need to prepare ourselves for the 21st century by making a commitment to *systematic, career-long learning*. This phrase is easy enough to say, but implicit in it is sacrifice. Reading, research and thinking take time and effort. Most people can devote some of their leisure time to the pursuit of knowledge, but for it to be really effective they must also devote a significant part of their working time to it as well. For this to be possible there must be not only greater investment by companies in training and education but corporate cultures that value intellectuals. And those corporate cultures must accept that sometimes the most effective work anyone does occurs when they are sitting, staring out of the window, and thinking.

Accepting all this is the first step towards acquiring the power that knowledge will bring in the 21st century. At the same time we need to recognise that, once knowledge becomes the source of real power in the society, then not only our corporate cultures but also our legal systems and their priorities are going to change.

Stop, thief! Give me back my ideas!

If we were asked to nominate the one thing that has differentiated Western capitalist society from other societies throughout history, that thing would most probably be the rule of law. Ultimately it is the rule of law which protects the Western way of life, even from the threats of parliaments that imagine they can legislate to achieve any end they want. Much of the legal thinking which underpinned the law's evolution was related to protecting people's rights—particularly their rights to property. Even when property was predominantly physical—goods, chattels and land—the law was complex. Now we face an infinitely more complex situation because of the knowledge revolution that the millennium will bring.

The Australian Institute of Management's chief executive, Peter Sheldrake, says that dealing with knowledge and using knowledge in business are quite different from dealing with physical objects or physical services. In the *Business Review Weekly*, in August 1995, he said: 'Knowledge is a much more slippery subject to deal with. It has characteristics that are quite different to those [of] physical objects. The conventional story is that you can always sell knowledge, but you still have it when you have sold it'.

The problem in the new millennium is going to be to devise laws to ensure that we do actually still own some rights to knowledge after we have sold it or after it has been dispatched into cyberspace.

One of the most difficult issues facing the final round of GATT negotiations, which preceded the creation of the new World Trade Organisation (WTO), was how to deal with intellectual property. Pierre Cardin, visiting Indonesia, said he must have at least 50 Indonesian namesakes—judging from the range of goods sold there under his name but without his authority. In Bangkok and Bali, in China and Chiapasa, it is possible to buy fake Gucci watches, Lacoste shirts and tapes of everything from the latest Batman movie to the latest pop song.

The piracy of software is a huge industry too. A Microsoft lawyer has estimated that piracy results in lost revenue for software firms of more than $200 million a year. This is almost certainly an underestimate. It has been claimed that this could be the loss that American companies experience in Italy alone each year. *The Economist* of 13 January 1996 reported that the University of Salerno had estimated that counterfeit business in Italy produced about $1 billion worth a year of goods ranging from tapes to handbags and clothing. And in 1995 Italian authorities seized 130 000 items of counterfeit Louis Vuitton goods and materials in raids on street vendors and backyard manufacturers.

The developed world is trying hard to ensure that intellectual copyright laws are internationally respected. The on-going trade friction between the United States and China has constantly been exacerbated by the United States' belief that the Chinese tolerate piracy. During 1995 the Chinese authorities launched a number of high profile raids on pirate tape production firms to indicate that it intended to address the issue. The problem came to the fore again in 1996. Australia has signed an intellectual property agreement with Vietnam which is designed to facilitate co-operation between the two countries. Under the agreement there will be technical workshops, exchange of officials and the like to ensure that the WTO's Agreement on Trade-Related Aspects of Intellectual Property Rights is properly implemented.

But the issue is not just one of piracy. Questions of intellectual copyright are becoming more and more complex because of technological change. If we think for a moment of what the multimedia revolution has in store for us, we can see how horrendously complex some of the problems are. Someone sits at a computer terminal in the office and connects to the Internet. They link up to a database which provides them with information about designs in a specific area. To obtain more information they pull more and more items out of the database: an image of a pattern contained in a museum in Florence; a few biographical details about the designer from a book in the US Library of Congress; some critical works from another source in the British Library; some images from the British National Gallery's CD-Rom of its collection of paintings. A person sitting at a desk can obtain dozens of items—all of which have some intellectual property rights. How do the owners get recompensed, and how are their rights protected?

Australia has been a leader in addressing intellectual property rights. It was the first country to introduce Public Lending Right—a system under which authors are reimbursed for each occasion one of their books is borrowed from a public library. It is, as Sheldrake put it, a case of selling the property but keeping it. The book is sold to a library but the rights of usage—the benefits of the intellectual property—still reside with the owner. The system has now been extended to educational libraries through Educational Lending Right.

New attempts are being made in Australia to define moral rights for artists and authors to enable them to protect their rights over the integrity and usage of their works. The Australian Law Reform Commission is also reviewing the Designs Act—passed in 1906—to improve regulation, protection and dispute resolution in the field of design rights.

Michael Fraser, chief executive of Australia's Copyright Agency Limited, is a leading international proponent of the need for new approaches to cross-border distribution and copyright fees. He points out that most copyright has been based on the printed word and says that 'authors' relationships with their writings, their publisher and their readers will alter as words enter space. Words will not only be distributed on the pages of a book, but will be available as an information product or on-line or on demand in chapter portions or snippets'.

In this new environment conventional copyright law will be inadequate and new intellectual property laws—technology-neutral laws—will need to be evolved.

New approaches to accounting will also be required. Most of the systems for dealing with accounting for intellectual property are as primitive as the accounting for Hollywood films. To give one example: *The Guardian* in the United Kingdom reveals that Winston Groom, author of the novel *Forrest Gump*, made about $350 000 from selling the film rights. He accepted the $350 000 lump sum and was to get a third of the net profits. So far, the film has taken some $600 million worldwide. But—when all costs were taken into account—it had made a $62 million loss! With the rapid evolution of the multimedia industry, more such episodes will occur, prompting more debate, and more disputes, about intellectual property and accounting methods.

The more the new millennium makes knowledge the basis of success the more the opportunity for dispute about who owns what and how it is used. For centuries budding lawyers have thought of the law relating to land and commerce as the domain in which they could find guaranteed prosperity. In the new millennium it will be electronic commerce and intellectual property that could well be the path to a legal earnings nirvana.

Innovations, transformations and revolutions

What do Americans think has been the most significant technological advancement of the past 25 years? Pause for a moment to think of the advances made in computing, telecommunications, aerospace and biotechnology, and the possibilities are endless. Yet, when they were asked by a market research company, Briskin-Goldring, in its Seiko Kinetic Countdown Survey, the answer was . . . the microwave oven.

Reporting the survey results in the 3 November 1995 issue of *Research Report,* Briskin-Goldring said that 63 per cent of those surveyed said the microwave oven had the most significant impact on their everyday lives. Cable television was the next most influential, with 43 per cent saying it had a significant impact. These were followed by answering machines 35 per cent, video cassette recorders 32 per cent, automated teller machines 28 per cent—and the computer . . . just 29 per cent.

The research firm concluded that the findings show that time represents freedom to Americans and that they value technology that gives them more of it. In this situation the microwave is valued not because it cooks meals but because it is about time. The computer is less important because—while many use one daily—it is seen as a business tool and not a convenience in their daily lives.

There are a number of other conclusions, however, which can be drawn from the findings. The first is that, for most people, 'significance' relates solely to their daily lives. While this seems so painfully obvious as to be banal, we constantly lose track of its importance. Those involved in creating or marketing technology are often enthused by the sheer beauty of the technology or the process, and expect others to react in the same way. The telecommunications engineer, for instance, expects people to gasp at the sophisticated technology which makes it possible to route calls and data around the world. In fact, people don't go around exclaiming 'gee whiz' whenever they turn on the light, switch on the television or pick up the telephone. Instead they quickly adapt to the changes the technology brings, and then take them for granted.

The second conclusion is that people don't actually visualise many transforming technologies other than when they can tangibly relate to them. The respondents to the Briskin-Goldring survey said the computer was significant but saw it only as a tool they used at the office. Yet all the products and services they listed as significant are, in fact, part of the computer revolution. The convenience of the ATM is dependent on the computing power employed by banks, but the respondents didn't make that connection. Equally they don't think of various services as computer-driven. When they make an airline reservation they think about the airline, the destination and the standard of customer service. They don't think about the global telecommunications and computing power which make it possible.

But, while it is surprising that those Americans who were surveyed chose the microwave oven as the most significant technology of the past quarter of a century, it is almost certain that a survey in another 25 years time will throw up an equally surprising result. The reason is that we are going through not just a profound change in society but a period in which the rate of technological change is even more massive than the breathless technocrats are suggesting.

Innovation in the earlier Industrial Revolution was often purpose-driven. In the British cotton industry in the 18th century a series of innovations came from the need to spin cotton faster, weave it faster and make it into garments faster. The innovations did not come as a totality but as individual initiatives by inventors such as Arkwright and Cartwright, who set out to solve a specific problem raised by some other innovation.

Side by side with industrial innovation was a transformation in agriculture—again brought about by people purposefully searching out, and experimenting with, better agrarian practices. Most of the people involved in this transformation were simple, practical people with little contact with the ruling classes or the universities. One exception was King George III—a most successful agricultural innovator. The universities were far more concerned with philosophical issues or pure research.

Today, governments in countries such as Britain and Australia are again fighting the 18th century battles in the course of restructuring tertiary education and research in order to focus them more strongly on practical outcomes and economic benefits. The great irony is that—as the new millennium approaches—we are moving once more into an era when the serendipitous outcomes from pure research will probably be far more significant than the purpose-driven research beloved of governments.

The best example of the virtues of such serendipity is the Internet. Almost everyone appears to be aware of the Internet today, although the number of users is still only about 30 million and most of those are male, aged over 25 and American. What is not so well known is exactly what the Internet is, how it has grown and how it represents an alternative vision for the future to that being pursued by governments and large companies.

The Economist of 1 July 1995 summed up the most important feature of the Internet when it dubbed it 'the accidental superhighway'. *The Economist* said:

> For almost all of its 25 year life this loose confederation of interconnected networks has been the arcane domain of computer scientists and academics, a private line for electronic conversation that no one else would understand anyway. The Internet's builders laid no cables and dug no trenches: they simply leased existing telephone lines.

But in 1993 the Internet was transmogrified into 'cyberspace'—a new, interactive multimedia network. It was still the same network, but others began to see its potentialities and suddenly it became the fastest growing communications and consumer electronics technology the world had ever seen.

At the same time as the Internet has been developing, cable and telephone companies have been working to wire the world. Optical fibre cable is being delivered to more and more premises, opening up the wondrous possibility of fifty or sixty versions of the pap that we currently see on television each night. The telephone and cable companies, however, promise more than just re-run movies. The great potential for cable, they say, will come with interactivity. In Australia, Optus Vision, Apple Computer, Springfield Land Corporation and advertising agency George Patterson Bates have combined to create a new 18 000 hectare site just outside Brisbane. Every home, business and community facility in Springfield will be equipped with a computer and wired with optical fibre cabling to an enormous community network. Electronic mail, bulletin boards, television, medical information and educational material will all be available.

Yet, as *The Economist* says: 'The Internet already offers most of the services and technologies that cable and telephone companies are still a decade from delivering. You can make a telephone call; watch a video; listen to an audio broadcast, or broadcast yourself; shop; learn and, of course, communicate'.

This is not to argue that optical fibre cabling is not going to deliver wonderful opportunities. Rather, it illustrates the fact that much of the current debate on the next transformational technology—the fusion of computing and telecommunications—is about technology which is actually a quarter of a century old, and which is already delivering many of the benefits we are promised for the 21st century.

To envisage the next transformational technology, therefore, we must look both further and elsewhere.

Nicholas Negroponte, Director of the Massachusetts Institute of Technology's Media Lab and author of the bestselling *Being Digital*, is one who looks further. He says that 'computing is not about computers, it's about life'. He says of the digital revolution:

> My intuition is that it is the big one, much bigger than the Industrial Revolution. But it's like a storm when you are in it—you really can't compare it so easily with other storms. My guess is that the implications of this revolution—because of its global nature—will force major changes in nationalism, education and economics.

Negroponte generates provocative ideas at a staggering pace. His most important insight may be, however, that the technology itself is transformational in ways we simply cannot anticipate.

But looking elsewhere, as well as further, allows us to see that, although most of the current debate about transformational technology is heavily focused on the digital revolution, there are other revolutions—as in biotechnology—also going on. In the case of biotechnology the revolution is now almost 50 years old. But the pace of change since the double helix breakthrough is rapidly accelerating. It may well be that some biotechnological breakthrough in agriculture or medicine will be the technology we look back on in the 21st century and see as the most crucial.

In the 19th century it was the steam engine and the railway; in the 20th century it has been the automobile and the convergence of computing and telecommunications. In the new millennium it will most probably be something which we have not yet envisaged. It is this fundamental uncertainty which requires us, as we will see in Chapter 6 and 7, to adopt new approaches to marketing and business planning.

Communications technology is useless without content

One of the most infuriating things about visiting friends in the United States is cable television. Well, not cable television itself, but the ritual of being introduced to it.

The encounter starts with your friends saying: 'You must see this . . . there's nothing like it anywhere else in the world'. They then proceed to zap the television screen to show you the 40 or 50 channels available. The remarkable thing is that as you flip from channel to channel you notice something extraordinary—all the individual contents begin to merge into each other. There are endless news and current affairs programs discussing the same narrowly focused group of current United States topics. There are the same politicians and political commentators elevating some obscure symbolic action above substance. There are all the television programs you loved as a child, and all the films you saw on Saturday afternoons at the cinema. The only relief comes from the excruciatingly amateurish, or the astonishingly bizarre, offerings of some public television channels.

As you watch politely, the events and images become disconnected from reality, and you begin to realise why United States foreign policy, say, or business investment strategy, tends to dwell on the short term. Everyone's attention span has been progressively eroded as they are bombarded with disparate bits of information day in and day out.

It might well be fascinating to watch a United States Congressional inquiry on cable television. The Public Broadcasting System's program on the Civil War might be one of the finest pieces of television made anywhere in the world. But the vast majority of material on cable is no different from what we get on most network television stations.

The point is that the most wonderful communications technology is useless without content.

Media companies the world over have already recognised this. The BBC—regarded as one of the best broadcasters in the world—in fact pushes out a steady diet of comedy and sport. The BBC's reputation these days is based primarily on a few outstanding nature shows and on a series of adaptations of classic English literature. In other words, its reputation for quality has little to do with technology and much to do with the fact that it operates in a milieu that can readily draw on Jane Austen, George Eliot and Shakespeare.

In the United States the merger mania between telephone and cable companies is being matched by the merger mania among media companies. In 1995 Walt Disney and Capital Cities/ABC merged. Time Warner—of Warner Music, Warner Bros films, Home Box Office and Time Magazine—has the second largest cable network and yet it wants to merge with

Ted Turner's CNN. And Japanese electronic companies such as Sony have taken over various Hollywood entertainment companies in order to have a readymade source of content.

Already the average man, woman or child in the United States is estimated to spend about nine hours a day listening to, reading and watching various media. About one hour of the nine is spent with print and the rest with electronic media. Spending on cable service, music recordings, newspapers, magazines, books, cinema and home video movies is about 75 cents per capita per day.

Satisfying this demand has created a massive cultural industry. But the most remarkable thing about this industry is that at its base there is always one thing of overriding significance—human creativity. Even soap operas and games shows need creative people to write scripts, develop scripts and package the show. Even the most desensitised media junkie occasionally needs stimulus beyond the flickering of the screen. And even the tiredest business person collapsing in front of the television late at night sometimes needs more than the screen watching them as they nod off in the chair.

For the cultural industry this creates a fascinating contrast with other industries. The workers within the industry can be all-powerful. Stars, talented directors, talented writers can never be dispensed with, because ultimately the content that attracts audiences depends on them.

Some years ago one of Australia's long established broadsheet newspapers, the Melbourne *Age*, was taken over and a new management installed. One of the first priorities for the new management was to change the paper's culture and to ensure that managers managed and that the authority of journalists was reduced. The new management remarked that the lunatics had been allowed to run the asylum. The management was successful in its bid to get control. But very rapidly the readership began to decline and community complaints reached a crescendo as the newspaper lost its way, its focus and its soul.

The cultural industries are the same: while the lunatics are in charge they prosper. When the keepers decide that *they* know best—and try to wrest back control—they decline.

That is the reality the telecommunications and cable television companies must face in the new millennium. However sophisticated their technology, their success in attracting audiences will still depend on how well those creative lunatics perform! And it is that reality which will provide the impetus for the millennium's fastest growing industry.

The millennium's Michelangelos—the coming global Renaissance

In the 1890s Australia was the richest country in the world on a per capita basis. The nation had abundant natural resources which could be supplied at competitive prices, and labour shortages pushed up wages.

For much of the 20th century many Australian commentators bemoaned our decline from this position. In the 1980s every drop in an OECD ranking was seen as a failure of government and of Australians at large, who had failed to recognise the hard world in which they lived and had failed to adapt to it as quickly as they should have.

The decline was often contrasted with the miraculous growth of Singapore—where a united, clever and hardworking nation, without natural resources beyond the wit and intelligence of its workforce, prospered. Singapore's then leader, Lee Kuan Yew, used to cite Australia as a dire warning as to what could happen if Singaporeans relaxed their commitment to work. Today Singapore has become a First World country and now its high standard of living is leading its citizens to question whether the Lee Kuan Yew way is necessarily the best.

The point of this comparison is very simple. Australia was the first country in the world to experience almost universal affluence. The affluence was relative—there was poverty—but there was no doubt that Australia was rich, successful and offered its people a good life. Even today, United Nations indicators make it clear that Australia is one of the world's best places to live in.

Being the first place to experience this new affluence, Australia was also the first place to begin to yearn for a different sort of life. The fact that Singapore is now experiencing exactly the same thing suggests that it may be more a product of affluence than a product of geography, ethnicity or culture.

And, in an affluent society, people's need for more than just work is what drives the growth of the cultural industries.

Following Federation in 1900, 217 museums and art galleries have opened, according to Australian Bureau of Statistics (ABS) reports on Australian culture in the 1990s. More than half of these—129—opened since 1980. With a population well below 20 million, in 1992–1993 the country produced 24 feature films, 92 independent television documentaries, 38 independent television miniseries and ten telemovies. In the same period 1 135 820 people visited the National Gallery of Australia in the national capital, Canberra. In other words, about one in 17 Australians travelled to a remote capital city with a small resident population—a sort of clean and pleasant Brasilia—and visited the art gallery. Other galleries had similar attendances, with the principal Queensland and Victorian galleries attracting three-quarters of a million visitors each and the galleries in Adelaide, Perth and the Victorian provincial town of Ballarat attracting more than half a million visitors each.

The *Australian Year Book 1995*—produced by the ABS—demonstrates how popular a wide range of cultural activities are. Attendances at museums and art galleries totalled 6.5 million in 1990–91; more than eight million attended performances of theatre, opera, music theatre, dance, and symphonic, chamber and choral works. More than 3 million attended both dance and classical music performance. The total revenue of all music and performing arts organisations was almost $300 million and the value of all audiovisual production—including films—was more than $1.2 billion. Australians are also among the world's heaviest readers of books.

The crucial fact about this flourishing artistic life is that Australia has never been a particularly intellectual country. It has beaches and a wonderful outdoor life to attract those who want more than work. It was Australia, after all, that first produced the bumper sticker, 'I'd rather be sailing'—and the nation has always been one in which sport is regarded as more important than culture. Indeed, many other countries—some considerably poorer—have higher participation in the arts and culture than Australia does. In terms of art and art museum attendances Australia ranks 37th in the world. At 360 attendances per thousand head of population, Australia ranks lower than Hungary (1800), the United States (1500), Canada (640), Brunei (510) and Iceland (462).

What the Australian example tells us, however, is that there is a link between increasing affluence and a tendency to consume more products of the cultural industries. In the new millennium, it is almost certain, the standard of living of a huge number of the world's population—particularly in the Asia–Pacific region—is going to improve. When it does, we can confidently expect that they, like Australians, will begin to look for more than work and materialism and will start to explore cultural opportunities.

The Australian example has another lesson for us as well. The growing interest in arts and culture in Australia has been linked to another phenomenon—the search for an Australian identity. Most Australian arts were imported from other cultures—particularly European cultures. In the 1970s Australians began to look to their own culture as a means of defining an Australian identity in a complex world. We have already noted that growing alienation will be one of the characteristics of society in the 21st century, and that people will respond to that alienation by searching for a sense of security and belonging. It is inevitable therefore that, as globalism increases, more nations will seek to glorify and celebrate their own culture in exactly the same way. As their standard of living increases—and as the demand for cultural product increases—so more people will seek to meet it.

Canada, for instance, has always had writers, but it is only as the country has become more closely tied to the United States economically that the flowering of literature represented by Alice Munro, Mordechai Richler and Margaret Atwood has emerged. Roper Starch Worldwide, a market research firm, conducted a survey in 40 countries. It found that 62 per cent of respondents felt that their culture would be increasingly influenced by American films and television . . . and 60 per cent didn't like it. Furthermore, it found that some 79 per cent of Central Europeans actually hated the idea. Sentiments of this kind will encourage local film production in such countries as much as the North American Free Trade Agreement is encouraging Canadian writers.

And finally—as a product of affluence—more people are going to have more leisure. While some in the West have worked longer hours in the last decade, this reduction in leisure time is insignificant compared with the liberation of peasants from the fields, which economic change is bringing about in the emerging world.

Taken together with the proliferation of communication technologies, these trends point to a gigantic explosion in demand for the products and services of the cultural industries. Businesses which serve the cultural industries—or can link their activities to them through sponsorships and philanthropy—can be among the beneficiaries of a global cultural renaissance which may do more to transform the world than even technology will do.

5 Communicating with Generation MM

The biggest difficulty facing 20th century generations in visualising what the new millennium might bring is the extent to which their ideas about the 21st century have been shaped by popular culture and science fiction.

In the 1980s I visited Brasilia, the Brazilian capital created in the middle of the country as the symbol of a new era allegedly dawning in Latin America. Brasilia is one of those immensely visionary—but immensely flawed—attempts at modernistic town planning. Although it is difficult to see except in schematic form, the city is laid out in the shape of a plane. Not just any plane, but the architect's vision of what a 21st century plane would look like. In fact it looks very much like a 1950s science fiction vision of a plane instead of the stubby, rocket-like ones which have been developed.

In approaching the 21st century we can easily make the same mistake. We can focus on technology, on the modern, on the futuristic—all from our own viewpoint—and miss the reality. This mistake is likely to be most pronounced in relation to assumptions about how we can communicate with Generation MM. It is easy to extrapolate a vision in which Generation MM sits at a terminal, surfing the information distributed throughout cyberspace. And yet . . . in a society in which values and human interaction are important, will things be exactly as we imagine?

Stop talking *at* people and start talking *with* them

A significant amount of business communication is designed to persuade people to do something. It may be a message from the CEO about the need for the organisation to become more competitive. It may be a marketing message designed to persuade someone to try a new product. It may also be a political message designed to persuade someone to vote in a different way.

Most of these communications are one-way. We send the message out and (apart from some market research or sales data) we tend not to receive messages back. We don't know, because we don't have inbuilt feedback in the process, precisely what message has been received.

Far too often we do know that the message has not prompted the outcome we anticipated. Part of the reason rests with a phenomenon we have all experienced. It is known as cognitive dissonance. The phenomenon occurs because we tend to filter new information through our existing knowledge, attitudes and prejudices. If the new information doesn't fit with these existing 'cognitions' we try to reduce the resulting dissonance, because it is unpleasant. A smoker who does not want to stop smoking, for instance, will tend to ignore the scientific evidence on its links with cancer, and will selectively grasp at anything that might suggest that smoking is not harmful.

Cognitive dissonance applies all the time in normal life. We just have to stop to think for a moment about how the problem is compounded when we bombard people with information. We are already doing so through media messages, advertising, conversations, exhortations, memos and so on. The more the information the greater the likelihood of it being filtered. In the next millennium the range of communication technologies is going to expand even more rapidly. People will be surrounded by the noise of communications.

In many cases they will just switch off; or, if they do absorb information, it will be through the cognitive dissonance filter.

Whenever a politician appears on television the vast majority of the audience doesn't hear what he or she is really saying—they interpret the politician's words and presentation in the context of their basic attitude to him or her. If a company has a poor corporate image, its protestations about how it has become more ethical are unlikely to be heard. Instead, receivers of the message will tend to take something from it that reinforces their belief about the company.

However, once we understand what cognitive dissonance is, and how it affects the receipt of our messages, we can begin to take a new approach to communication. This new approach involves ensuring that all our communication processes are two-way and they are followed by a conscious effort to determine that we have been heard.

In the millenarian age there will be many people who sincerely believe that no one is listening to them and no one is really trying to communicate with them. Indeed, most of the efforts to reach them will merely reinforce the problem. The company that breaks through the noise—overcomes the dissonance—and demonstrates that it is listening, as well as telling, will reach its audience. And breaking through the noise will increasingly be the result of choosing the right channel through which to target the audience.

People trust the information that comes from the channels they trust

Many years ago a marketing experiment was carried out in two Canadian provinces. In one province a product was launched using advertising only. In the other province the same product was launched without advertising but with extensive media coverage generated by public relations efforts.

After the products had been launched researchers went out to customers and asked where they had heard about the product. In the province where advertising had been used for the launch, the majority of respondents said they had read about the product in the newspapers. In the province where the newspaper launch was used, the majority of respondents said they had seen some advertising about it.

The results don't, in fact, indicate that advertising and media relations don't work. What they indicate is that people are not always totally sure where they got their information from. It's hardly surprising, given the barrage of noise and messages we are all faced with every day. In fact, we now know, from research in many different markets, that the most likely source of information about a new product is a friend, a family member or some other communication channel that the consumer trusts and respects.

The editor of Australia's *Marketing Magazine*, Michael Kiely, gives three examples of this process. A United States computer services company polled 100 new customers to find out why they became customers. Only 5 per cent mentioned advertising, about 20 per cent mentioned a sales presentation, and 56 per cent came as a result of a referral by a colleague. The international market research company, Mintel, surveyed 7000 people in Europe to find out what made them try new products—60 per cent said recommendations by family and friends. The best example of all is the liqueur, Bailey's Irish Cream. Only 5 per cent of people try it for the first time because they respond to the ads promoting it; 64 per cent try it at the urging of their friends.

This word-of-mouth endorsement is powerful for two reasons. First, with products there are always 'early adopters'—people who try things, who experiment. The bulk of consumers are followers—they wait until an early adopter has validated a product. Second, there are communication networks in society which are not necessarily penetrable by normal means. In Australia the top-selling beer was always Fosters Lager. The beer was regarded as *the* Australian beer, and the brand was regarded as the people's brand. After the takeover of Fosters by John Elliott the company began to talk about 'Fosterising' the world. They made it clear that they saw the Fosters brand as the company's brand—not the people's. Gradually, and then at an accelerating rate, word-of-mouth networks spread a new message: 'Fosters isn't ours, so we won't drink it any more'. Instead, the population turned to another product—Victoria Bitter. Despite the lack of marketing support for this brand it became Australia's biggest selling beer. Fosters is still the world's favourite lager but it is no longer Australia's . . . and won't be until the company devises a way of giving the brand back to the consumer.

What is most important, however, is that during the entire process neither Fosters nor its competitors could work out exactly why the marketplace change was occurring. Yet the reason was obvious—the change was a product of community networking rather than traditional marketing.

People also turn to communication channels they trust because they are totally confused by the messages being sent. *PR Reporter*, in April 1995, recounted how CBD Research & Consulting of New York had probed the various competitive messages coming from telephone companies. Fully 78 per cent of the 1000 survey respondents said they were sick and tired of all the advertising and hype from United States telephone companies. The feeling was strongest among those with incomes of more than $50 000 a year (89 per cent) and among those in the 18–34 age group (83 per cent)—the two groups who are important markets for long distance phone services. The surveys also showed that 59 per cent were confused about available calling plans and that 60 per cent felt all the major providers charged the same, even though a majority also recognised that you could save money by choosing the right calling plan. Not only had the communication confused the consumer but it had even ended up contradicting what the consumer knew to be reality—that you could get cheaper calls.

How then can you cut through the confusion and barrage and find the channels which work?

The first way is to understand that in confusing times—such as a millenarian age—the most important communication paths are community networks. These can be extraordinarily disparate. In the case of young women with young children, the most effective networks might be found through infant welfare services, preschool committees and playgroups. With older people it may be elderly citizens' clubs.

I have a 21-year-old son who, when he lived with us, gave me advice on youth aspects of communication work—in return for food, shelter and access to a computer! At the time my company had been retained to develop a program, for a world computer games championship, for Blockbuster Video. The criterion for success was the number of people we got to sign up for the games. The questions that arose were: who is likely to sign up, where do we find them and how do we reach them? It was fairly obvious that the *Financial Review* and the *Wall Street Journal* were not the answer.

So I raised the question with my son, who looked at me with contempt and told me the answer was simple. You get some teenagers to go around to all the video games parlours and hand out leaflets. It wasn't a terribly sophisticated communication strategy, but it did turn out to be very good advice. We reached the audience we wanted to in a credible way—and achieved the result—because we found the right channel and a network the audience would trust.

We found exactly the same thing with communication campaigns for Telstra, the Australian telecommunications corporation, and the Department of Immigration and Ethnic Affairs.

In the first case, Telstra was facing the consequences of the first deregulatory decision made by the Australian Government. We needed to explain the decision and to ensure that the corporation maintained as much market share as possible in a field in which they had once had a total monopoly. We went about the communication by creating a 'family'—a group of people who matched the age, gender and background of the various sections of the markets that were most vulnerable. Then we sent them to schools, to elderly citizens' clubs, to service clubs and so on, and let them communicate the information to people who were just like them and therefore more likely to trust them.

With the immigration campaign, we needed to persuade residents of Australia to take up citizenship. In this case we chose ambassadors from each ethnic group affected and sent them out to ethnic festivals, clubs and gatherings. Immediately a record number of people applied to take out citizenship. The campaign was a success because it chose networks that people trusted, and sent messages into the networks through people the networks trusted.

In the new millennium there is going to be massive distrust. The population will be susceptible to extremist appeals from all sorts of groups. If business is to ensure that it is heard amidst the noise and babble of millenarian confusion, it will need to choose the right channels through which to send out its messages—the channels that people trust. One of them will involve a communications technique that the late 20th century assumes is dead and buried.

Show you really care—send a handwritten note

Modern historians often bemoan the fact that no one writes letters now. Brought up on a diet of documents, they find it hard to track down evidence in a society in which people use the telephone more often than the post. Around the world archivists and historians are seeking to ensure that the protection of government records extends to e-mail and the other electronic messages which tend to dominate communication today.

Already most companies use information technology (IT) extensively in communication. A 1995 survey made by Xerox and Cognitive Communications of the *Fortune* 100 (a list of companies) found that:

- 98 per cent use IT for disseminating information

- 47 per cent use it as a quick, convenient way to get feedback from employees
- 36 per cent use it to store information
- 29 per cent use it for information retrieval
- 16 per cent use it for collaboration

They use it because:

- 96 per cent say it shortens the communication cycle time
- 64 per cent say it reduces communication costs
- 53 per cent say it has increased distribution

E-mail is by far the most popular technique:

- 90 per cent use it for person-to-person communication
- 67 per cent use it for electronic publishing
- 54 per cent use it for online bulletin boards

Only one-third of the companies have a formal policy governing e-mail (privacy, information ownership, graphic formatting, distribution limitations and so on).

Other methods being used are:

- video conferencing (53 per cent)
- audio conferencing (51 per cent)
- broadcast voice mail (50 per cent)
- broadcast fax (47 per cent)
- fax-on-demand (36 per cent)
- live broadcast television (29 per cent)
- taped television (20 per cent)
- groupware (11 per cent) (this integrates work groups so that communication barriers disappear and collaboration across the enterprise becomes possible; while still relatively new, it's having a significant impact within organisations that use it)
- CD-Rom (3 per cent)
- desktop video (2 per cent)

Respondents predict that in three years time they will be using electronic and print methods equally often for internal communications: 42 per cent print and 41 per cent electronic.

In 1995, 57 per cent is print, 20 per cent electronic, 22 per cent video, 18 per cent face-to-face.

With e-mail the proliferation of messages is forcing more and more companies to develop codes of etiquette and policies to make its use more effective. The recipient of a message that has got a whole series of other people's comments tacked on to it can be bewildered by the range and volume of information. Whereas once people complained of clearing the paper from their desk, they now complain of having to clear their screen of e-mail messages.

Direct mail technology is also allowing companies to target individuals. Telemarketing means that most people get regular calls from people asking them questions, selling them products and services, and treating them like an individual they know well.

In companies the most effective way of cutting through the clutter is to ensure that face-to-face communication remains the primary source of interaction between people. I have a colleague who refuses to read her e-mail. She reasons that if the message is important enough the person will telephone, or walk around to her desk, to talk about it. She also reasons that her time is too valuable to wade through all the extraneous messages which come in. She also says that e-mail lacks the personal touch—the courtesy—of going out of your office to *talk* with an individual rather than just sending a few words off into cyberspace.

But unfortunately you can't just walk down the corridor when offices are a world apart. And London people can't talk to the other side of the world whenever they feel like it, because someone on the other side of the world is likely to be asleep and to resent being woken up.

The end result is that we have wonderful communications technologies which link us all but which lack the personal touch and which run the risk of merging messages into the noise around them.

Many people also work directly to a screen and rarely use written notes. The most frequently used pen for these people is the marker pen. And managers carry their Mont Blanc pen and pencil sets in their briefcases, but make notes in their personal computer notebook. By the 21st century this trend will probably have become so pronounced that Generation MM will rarely see their own handwriting, let alone the handwriting of others.

In such a situation the handwritten note will assume a new significance. It will be a symbol of authenticity and an indication that the individual cares enough to take the trouble to write. It may be a quick, jotted note on a With Compliments slip or a scribble on the back of a business card attached to a package. And one of the few remaining uses for faxes not connected by modem to a computer will be sending handwritten notes faster than the mail service can.

We won't do it often because the effort will be too great. But when we really want to impress someone we'll pull out pad and pen, and sit down and write, to produce a document which demonstrates just how much we wanted the person to receive this particular message.

When Generation MM see a suit they will see a problem, not a solution

Christine Milne is now a Member of Parliament in Tasmania, Australia's island State. In the 1980s she lived on her farm in the north of the island. Close to where she lived, at Wesley Vale, a major pulp and paper company set out to build a pulp mill. This precipitated a major environmental and political battle. Christine Milne was an ordinary resident of the State with a passion for her area and an opposition to the company. The company had many highly trained spokespeople and sophisticated communications technology.

In the ensuing battle Christine Milne—and her supporters—won, and the company lost.

The victory raises another important question about communicating with Generation MM. As we have seen, the emphasis in such communication needs to be on dialogue, on establishing trust and on emphasising the personal. But it also raises questions about who has done most of the communicating in the 20th century and who will do it most effectively in the 21st century.

During the 1980s there were a great many of those who had been doing the communicating—company and industry association executives—who became frustrated, bitter and twisted about media interviews and environmental issues. Their experiences epitomise the problems that managers will experience in the 21st century unless they learn to understand the new values that Generation MM will espouse.

As the environmental tidal wave swept across the world, every day of the week seemed to see some new accusation about some industry or some company devastating the earth, destroying the last piece of wilderness in some nation or polluting the atmosphere. Time after time executives, who had been given extensive media and presentation training, were made to look like fools on television by bright young environmentalists.

Working with a number of companies that needed to communicate details of their environmental performance to the community, I began to wonder about the problem of why executives were not believed in environmental debates, and environmentalists were.

One possible explanation was that journalists tend to be iconoclastic and that their sympathies are by definition with the underdog. In fact, most journalists are not iconoclastic at all. Journalists are trained to give more credence to authority figures than to others. They are also more motivated by the prospect of a story getting 'a run', as they call it, thereby helping their egos and careers, than by the desire to destroy capitalism or embarrass some icon. A second explanation was that business—because of the excesses of the 1980s—was simply not trusted. It is true that attitudes to business during the period were cool, but business was no more seen as a specific problem than was government or a number of other institutions.

In fact, after pondering the problem for some time, it became clear that the real reason was to do with the differences between the executives and the environmentalists. Even though the executives were usually logical and well-briefed they did tend to be middle-aged, middle class males—*suits.* On the other hand, the environmentalists were typically idealistic and often female.

The problem was simple. Most middle-aged, middle class males in the 1980s tended to have a common characteristic—they were fathers. It sounds banal, but when you think about it you see the source of the problem. Fathers don't know the answers to school homework questions. Fathers can't fix the washing machine. Fathers get lost on outings in the car and are too stubborn to ask for directions. Fathers can't cook a meal without wrecking the kitchen. Yet here—on television screens around the world—were a flock of fathers saying the planet was safe, there was no environmental risk, and we really just had to have some faith. They were saying: 'We don't need to stop and ask for directions, because I'm sure if we just go down here we'll get back on the right road soon'.

The smart industry associations began to employ younger female executives. The most brilliant success in Australia was the appointment of a former federal government cabinet minister, Susan Ryan, as head of the Australian Plastics Industry Association. Susan was a leading feminist who had done an enormous amount to raise awareness of women's issues in politics. As head of the plastics industry she confronted a wide range of problems. The public found plastic products safe, convenient and reliable. Growth rates were steady as plastics were substituted for many other materials. Yet there were still nagging concerns. People worried about plastics in waste; they felt guilty about using them. They assuaged that guilt by recycling plastic supermarket bags and ice cream containers, but the guilt was regularly reignited by environmentalists to whom plastics were the personification of environmental evil.

A particular target of environmentalists was the disposable nappy, which used a considerable amount of plastic. The debate about disposable versus old-style nappies appears simple but is, in fact, an example of how complex many environmental questions are. There are difficult tradeoffs between water and energy usage and so on which complicate the question as to which is best. These complexities were too great for the media, and most of the publicity, fuelled by environmentalists, focused on how evil disposable nappies were.

Susan Ryan confronted the issue rationally by pointing out the complexities. But she also launched a pre-emptive strike. In a major speech to a conference on women and the environment she said that the argument about disposable nappies was part of a wider environmental problem. In almost every case where environmentalists posed a simpler, back-to-nature solution it involved a radical shift in responsibilities within households. Almost every labour-saving device and service that had liberated women from the drudgery of the home was under challenge. The disposable nappy debate was part of this campaign to undo the liberation and ensure that 'women went back to being barefoot, pregnant and beating the clothes on the rocks in the stream'.

The speech attracted enormous publicity and then, almost overnight, the disposable nappy debate ended. A middle-aged male arguing the economic and environmental facts could never have done it. And business must learn that in the 21st century they would be foolish to even try.

Giving a speech to the Australian Gas Association some years ago, I looked around the room and suddenly realised that the audience—some 250 people—were mostly male, and that nearly all of them were wearing blue or grey suits. There was just one table of women—and they were the AGA chief executive's personal assistant and the people who were handing out the name tags.

The topic I was addressing was communications in a complex society. But clearly the complexity had not yet reached into the gas industry's senior management levels. This was no fault of the industry as such, which has been well run and very profitable. It was a product of the background, education and age of the managers. Many of them were engineers who had graduated in an era in which, at most, only a handful of women were enrolled in engineering. Most of those in the audience had come to senior management positions via field assignments once considered unsuitable for women. And most of them wore blue or grey suits because it was the manager's uniform. Young executives are socialised in the workplace just as they are at school. At school they learn the rituals and language that allow them to fit in and get on. So it is in offices, where you quickly learn that suede brogues or brown suits are just not right.

This reality is reflected in statistics on the Australian workforce. The powerful jobs are still occupied by men and, of the top 2000 private sector managers in the country, only about 200 are women. At the same time, of the 2.6 million Australians employed in clerical and sales jobs women make up 1.9 million. In the skilled trades women account for just 10 per cent of the workforce.

The situation in small business is radically different—mainly because many women find that small business provides a more flexible lifestyle or gives them the opportunity to avoid problems of discrimination. In Australia women own nearly 50 per cent of sole-proprietor small businesses. According to the Australian Department of Industry, Science and Technology, up to 70 per cent of start-up businesses are owned by women. In all, women own between one-quarter and one-third of all small businesses.

The picture is broadly similar in the United States. Bloomberg Financial Services reports that in 1992 women owned 6.4 million firms—one-third of all United States firms—and employed 13.2 million workers. From 1987 to 1992 the number of women-owned firms grew by 43 per cent, almost double the rate of growth for all firms, with the exception of large corporations. According to the US National Association for Women Business Owners, one in every ten in the United States workforce is employed in female-owned companies.

In November 1994 Chris Lee, managing editor of *Training Magazine*, outlined some of the changes taking place in the wider business environment. In the United States, between 1979 and 1992, the number of women in the workforce grew at twice the rate of men. According to the US Bureau of Labor Statistics, 58 per cent of women over the age of 16 are now in the workforce, compared with 76 per cent of men. The BLS expects that by 2005 the figure for women will be about 65 per cent and for men still around 75 per cent. Of course this does not reflect the types of jobs being occupied; many of them are a result of the 'casualisation' of the workforce in the United States.

A more telling analysis, though, was carried out by the *Wall Street Journal*, which showed that, although women had only 21.7 per cent of management jobs in 1982, they held 30.5 per cent by 1992.

At board level in the United States things are also improving. The 1995 Catalyst Census, Multiple Women on Boards, found that more women are joining the boards of *Fortune* 500 companies. About 81 per cent of these companies have one or more women directors—up from 75 per cent in 1994 and 69 per cent in 1993. One-third of the companies have more than one female director, and the larger the company the higher the percentage of female directors. For instance, 95 per cent of the top 100 companies have women directors.

What is most pronounced is the fact that the women who are moving into management are now doing so on their own terms. In 1990 *Fortune* had said that women who wanted to succeed needed to 'look like a lady; act like a man; work like a dog'. A friend of mine working in human resources said he always—if most things were equal—chose the woman candidate, because she had to be smarter and to have worked harder to get into the position she had. The new shift in attitude was signalled by a controversial *Harvard Business Review* article written in 1990 by Judy N. Rosenberg, a professor at the University of California. In the article 'Ways Women Lead', she argued that women and men manage differently. About the same time, Sally Hegelsen's book *The Female Advantage*[28] appeared, arguing that women introduce networking and nurturing relationships into companies.

What women are saying is that they are different and that companies are stronger because they embrace and nurture such differences. The widespread use of mentoring is one practical example of this. Mentoring was rarely practised in management teams dominated by men, although it had always been a feature of the tradesperson/apprentice relationship. Today most companies committed to being learning organisations use mentoring as a way of encouraging the young and of passing on the experience and expertise of more senior managers. The better mentors, of course, also learn from those they are mentoring.

Companies are now systematically trying to develop the potential of women managers and many initiatives are underway to make it easier for women to fulfil their potential. In the longer term change will be accelerated by the fact that, in Generation MM, the numbers in tertiary institutions reflect a better gender balance in a wide range of disciplines. This means that the male dominance of management must come to an end in an economy where knowledge is the determinant of success.

But the change in management is not just about gender—it is also about class, age and ethnicity. When we say that this generation will be 'the last to be male' we can also assume that increasing cultural diversity means that it will the last to be mainly WASP—White Anglo-Saxon Protestant.

And when that day comes the symbol of today's manager—the suit—will probably also disappear. Taste, along with society, is being revolutionised. In countries like Australia men wore what they did because it was a uniform and a symbol that they had been socialised. In the past 20 years or so clothing companies such as Country Road have revolutionised men's attitude to clothing and fashion. They have made it permissible to be conscious of fashion and to adopt smart, casual clothes which match smart, casual lifestyles.

And already casual dress is becoming the norm for many American office workers. A survey made by Levi-Strauss and the Society for Human Resource Management shows that 90 per cent of the companies surveyed have some form of casual dress code for office workers. This compares with 63 per cent three years ago, when the first such survey was conducted. One-third of the companies allow casual dress every day, compared with 20 per cent in 1992. Some 42 per cent allow 'once a week' casual dressing—up from 17 per cent in 1992. Companies adopting the 'every day' code include IBM; and General Motors in Detroit is among the 'once a week' set. Most significantly, 85 per cent of managers said they believed casual dress codes improved office morale.

So, just as the men at the Australian Gas Association took their blue suits for granted, so Generation MM will take their Country Road clothes for granted.

6 Targeting Generation MM

While Generation MM will mix mysticism with modern technology, and care about values and the environment, it will also be the biggest and most affluent consumer group the world has yet seen. As the Asia–Pacific 'tigers' boom, and as eastern European economies are transformed, there are going to be millions and millions more people with more disposable income than ever before.

That, at least, is one fact about the 21st century on which nearly all business observers agree.

The problem, however, is that as the 21st century world is transformed so will be the ways in which companies market to Generation MM. Generation MM won't be just a mass market consuming solely global brands. It will pride itself on its local pride. It will want brands to stand not just for glamour but also for values and value. And, because of the bewildering array of changes in communications technology, marketers will have to adopt new ways to reach it.

There are no global markets—only a series of niche markets

Many years ago we went out to buy a dozen eggs and a bottle of milk. Both are as close to universal products as you can imagine. Both are found in well over 90 per cent of Australian refrigerators and both are lifelong items—products used from infancy through to very old age.

Yet the remarkable thing about them both is the extent to which they have become customised. You can buy eggs in many forms—brown, white, free-range; packaged in plastic or recycled cardboard; in small, medium, large or very large sizes. You can buy low fat milk, extra cream milk or flavoured milk, in bottles, plastic packaging or cardboard.

Egg producers and milk manufacturers didn't develop this astonishing variety in order to grow the market—they developed it to maintain market share in a marketplace where niches are becoming more and more important. In the new millennium—when diversity is going to be one of the primary characteristics of the world—this trend will be accentuated.

This is not to say that there won't still be global brands. Coca-Cola, McDonalds, Disney and a few others will still be sold in almost every market in the world. But even these brands will be customised to local markets. The Nike company is one example of this. On the face of it, the brand's international marketing is remarkably consistent. Under a slogan which has become part of the language—'Just do it'—the company features athletic heroes, all with an irreverent, anti-establishment point of difference. Michael Jordan, Chicago Bulls spearhead, was the personification of this approach. Nike's number one position, however, is maintained by a very subtle merging of global and local campaigns. Part of this is achieved simply by signing up local sporting heroes in local markets and featuring them in advertising. A more significant difference lies in the style and nature of advertising directed towards particular markets. At a time when many global companies are merely reshooting commercials and showing them around the world, Nike recognises that diversity demands that they create special messages for each different local market.

Two other industries also indicate the extent to which niche markets are becoming important. Seemingly, nothing could be more basic than steel. Australia's biggest company, BHP, exports more than two-thirds of what it produces in Australia and 44 per cent of what it makes in Australia and New Zealand. BHP's chief executive officer, John Prescott, told *Institutional Investor* in January 1995:

> Our competitive advantage in steel is a unique range of products tailored to the requirements of a series of niche markets. We produce as large a range of products as any steel maker in the world—probably a larger range. Though we don't do some of the things that the major United States or Japanese companies do, overall we do a wider range of things than most companies. And we do them competitively.

In the beer industry, too, one company has tended to dominate local markets, but a number of factors are changing this. First, more international breweries are growing, by merger, takeover or strategic alliance. Second, tastes are changing and there is now more demand for a more diverse range of beers. The big volume products are still immensely important, but boutique beers and imported beers are of growing significance in every nation in the world markets.

There is also, of course, the perennial problem with global brands—some brands simply don't travel well. McDonalds is changing just about everything about its product in order to move into the Indian market, where religious feelings are intense and the cow is sacred. A major Spanish potato crisp is called boom—spelt b.u.m. Sic and Pschitt are French soft drinks. And Super Piss—spelt p.i.s.s.—is a very successful Finnish product for unfreezing car doors.

The worldwide tension between globalism and localism is the trend most responsible for this need to adapt global brands to local needs. But we should not forget that within national markets there is increasing diversity as well.

The prime example of this diversity comes from the multicultural aspects of most societies. In the United States a number of major marketing communication agencies have sought to establish a specific multicultural niche. Most of the big United States advertising and public relations companies now have Hispanic and African-American subsidiaries—recognising that to communicate with these minority groups requires specific skills and specific cultural sensitivity.

While big companies are moving into the field smaller companies are using their expertise to grow into other areas. Crawley Haskins—an African-American public relations firm in Philadelphia—was started by two African-Americans who had worked as marketers in large corporations. They saw the emerging niche and left corporate life to set up their own shop.

But the significant thing about their business strategy was that they had no intention of remaining within the niche. Certainly they intended to continue to be specialists in communication with African-American audiences, but they also intended to take that multicultural specialisation and extend it to other niche markets as well.

Australia is another market where multicultural communications are becoming more important. The country's most successful multicultural marketer is Joseph Assaf of the agency Ethnic Communications. Assaf says that the biggest mistake companies make when selling to ethnic consumers is to take existing material and just translate it into a foreign language. He told the *Business Review Weekly* (November 6 1995):

> It happens regularly, a company translates an ad without understanding the culture and the idiom of the ethnic group it is targeting and then can't understand why the ad flops. Companies should re-create, not translate, their Anglo campaigns and make them culturally relevant to ethnic consumers.

Assaf works with some of Australia's biggest companies, including Telstra and the AMP Society. He has conducted a range of campaigns, all based on very careful research. Ethnic Communications maintains 'market intelligence networks'—groups of researchers who are in regular contact with ethnic communities to monitor social and attitudinal changes and test products and services.

In 1994 Assaf devised a campaign for Telstra's phone card division by creating a phone card to mark the Chinese Year of the Dog. Following promotion in Chinese language media and through public relations, Telstra sold a quarter of a million cards in a fortnight. For AMP, a new corporate campaign was launched featuring a female Eurasian accountant giving advice to her male client. Nothing could symbolise more vividly the fundamental change going on in Australia—once a European, male-dominated society.

One of the most important elements in Assaf's success is the fact that he uses, besides the ethnic media, a wide range of ethnic community networks which reach out to the target audiences through channels they trust.

The remarkable thing about niche markets is that—once we begin to understand them—it is much easier to reach them today than ever before. Today flexible manufacturing and flexible service offerings allow us to customise products and services in a way never before possible. We can provide cars with a myriad of different accessories, or we can have a Vietnamese partner to serve the legal or accounting needs of the Vietnamese community. Today almost nobody would try to sell a United States product in Quebec without having the commercial in French and a presenter who related to the audience.

In the new millennium almost no one will succeed by trying to sell to the world without first taking into account the growing local differences. Fortunately, we will have technologies that will make that immeasurably easier—if we use them carefully.

The ultimate marketing breakthrough—one-to-one interactive marketing

Much marketing has been a monologue—marketers talking to or at customers—rather than a dialogue, or talking with customers in a two-way process. The reason for this is generally that the mass media we use to communicate to mass markets have been one-way media. While it is possible to build in response mechanisms to television, radio and print advertising, the mechanisms are normally a cut-out coupon or a free call number. They allow response to the communication rather than interactive communication.

Any mass media communication is fine with a largely homogeneous mass market. With diverse niche markets it can be clumsy and ineffective. This reality is already changing media spending patterns. In 1987 the Commercial Economic and Advisory Service of Australia (CEASA) began publishing details of revenues for both traditional and non-traditional media. Non-traditional media include sales promotions, support given to merchandising in grocery and other stores, retail catalogues, direct mail and other similar media. Traditional media comprise newspapers, magazines, television, radio, outdoor advertising and cinema.

The CEASA figures show that between 1987 and 1989 spending on both traditional and non-traditional media continued to increase. Traditional media went up from just over $5 billion annual spending to almost $5.8 billion. Non-traditional spending went from $3.6 billion to $4 billion. But in 1989 the trends diverged, with traditional media falling in every year until 1993 when they began to climb again—back to roughly where they were in 1987. At the same time non-traditional media continued to grow to the point where spending on them is now over $5 billion and equivalent to traditional media.

This change was fundamentally driven by increasing market diversity and the need to use different media to reach different markets. Now, overlaid on that imperative are the new technologies we have been discussing in this book. The Internet, cable television, interactive digital media are all opening up new opportunities for interactive communication with these diverse audiences. The ninth annual Veronis Suhler & Associates communications industry forecasts, reported in *Research Report* in August 1995, project 19.9 per cent annual growth in interactive digital media through to the eve of the new millennium.

The new technologies allow us to use a myriad of channels to reach diverse audiences. They are also linked to the computing power needed to manage massive databases. We already take for granted the airline customer service data bases which record all our preferences—seating, diet and so on. We take for granted the hotel chain's capacity to greet us—in most cities of the world—and sincerely ask about our preregistered preferences.

Now information technology and immense database management capability have come together to allow us to develop the ultimate in target market segmentation—the pitch to the individual rather than the group.

Much one-to-one marketing has been direct marketing through either direct mail or telemarketing. The personally addressed letter from the politician, or the store, no longer has a great capacity to surprise us. Some direct marketing material is tacky and shoddy and the image of the industry as a whole is correspondingly diminished.

The new individual marketing tools will, however, be qualitatively different. Because they will be interactive they will allow two-way communication between company and customer. A retail store will be able to advise a valued customer of specific sale offerings which meet their needs. It will be able to instantaneously adjust the offers according to the feedback it gets. Airline companies and hotels will be able to make special offers on passengers' most or least used destinations and then use the feedback to book flights and accommodation instantly.

Loyalty programs, besides restricting customer turnover by

encouraging customer loyalty, also provide a host of information about customers which allow tailored offers to be made to them and to be acted upon immediately through digital contact. This is a step beyond current home shopping toward the levels of personal service that, centuries ago, only aristocrats were able to receive.

In the new millennium this personal touch will be made even more important because of consumers' search for security and a sense of belonging. The new interactive one-on-one marketing allows companies to say to more and more customers that they are special individuals the company really cares about.

Most consumers will embrace these services even though, implicit in them, is a major threat to privacy. The creation of databases inevitably creates suspicion and fear and the existence and use of such databases will fuel feelings of anxiety and paranoia. There will also be legitimate concerns about privacy. No one wants anyone to know every detail of their lives and preferences. They want to be able, as we have seen, to draw a line around themselves.

Inevitably there will, as a result, be tension between the comfort and the unease created by database marketing. In most countries privacy legislation to protect the individual will be a high priority. Indeed, even those most in favour of restrictions on privacy laws can have mixed feelings about the issue. Speaking to a group of real estate agents about political lobbying, I was asked what could be done about pending privacy legislation. They were concerned that new legislation would inhibit their ability to obtain information about the creditworthiness of prospective tenants. We talked in general terms about the balance of rights and obligations between landlord and tenant. But the final decision, I suggested, would be based on the presumption that privacy was more important. To illustrate the point I asked those present to raise their hand if they thought it was reasonable for anyone to have access to all their credit card uses—with dates, times and so on. While I am sure they were a very upright and moral group, it was revealing that, after some moments of thought, not a hand was raised.

Generation MM, like the estate agents, will want all the

benefits that database management can bring but only so far as they know they can still draw a line around their privacy. They will consent to forgo their privacy for proven benefits—but the consent will be informed, confined and defined.

New ways to get new insights into new millennium markets

One of Australia's leading market researchers, Rod Cameron of the ANOP company, has spent a lot of his career researching in the political field. He has remarked that it is getting more difficult to measure real voting intention and even more difficult to measure what real issues are. In a Qantas inflight magazine in 1995 he said:

> People are full of prejudices, long-held beliefs and illogical attitudes and it takes time and considerable skill to unwind the knots of an individual's belief system. The identification of the real issues is equally important in the business world as it is in politics. Too often businesses are victims of simplistic studies that accentuate the obvious issues such as price without identifying the interconnections that may lead to a more complex and effective business/customer relationship.

It is this failure which has resulted in some spectacular market research disasters. The total budgets committed to research by agencies and clients amount to billions of dollars. Yet time and time again we fail to anticipate new developments or even accurately gauge how products and services will be received. Time and time again companies get surprised.

There are five famous market research failures which indicate how this happens.

The first was the research undertaken by Xerox into the photocopier. When it went out and asked secretaries whether they wanted photocopiers, or whether they wanted to continue using carbon paper, they opted for carbon paper.

The Walkman also did really badly. No one would possibly want something hanging on their ear as they walked around, and anyway the quality would be awful.

In the United Kingdom it had always been imagined that it would be hard to sell the English lager as opposed to traditional ales. Generally it was felt that the best chance would be a lager in a bottle with a German name which built on the fame, and recognised the quality, of German beers. Today the biggest selling lager in the United Kingdom is Fosters.

Finally, two political market research failures. In 1970 Ted Heath unexpectedly beat Harold Wilson for the British prime ministership, despite Wilson's having a massive lead in the polls. After the event a variety of explanations were put forward—low vote, the weather and so on. The reality was that it was the campaign in which Enoch Powell first played the race and migration card. When asked whether they supported Powell, Heath and the Tories, people immediately said no. When given the opportunity to cast a ballot in secret, a significant number of people voted against migration and Wilson—and *for* Powell and thus Heath. The miracle win of John Major over the Labour Party in 1992 was another example. The polls had Labour well in front, but the problem was that people weren't telling the truth. They were saying that they were happy to pay more tax and spend more on social security, while in fact they were totally opposed to extra taxes.

These market research projects failed not because of any inherent weaknesses in methodology but for two other, more powerful, reasons. First, consumers often can't define their need for a product or service until they see it and, second, respondents often don't tell researchers the truth.

In many cases—as with the Walkman—a giant leap of imagination is required, an entrepreneurial leap in which we take a risk on what the consumer will want, rather than simply giving her or him more of the same in terms of incremental product enhancements, brand extensions or simple repackaging.

If we don't take the leap of imagination, we remain fixed on present behaviours—particularly mass behaviours—and the present, even while we are talking about it, becomes the past. We walk into the future backwards.

This phenomenon is going to be even more pronounced as the new millennium unfolds. As more and more people are exposed to market research they will get better and better at hiding what they think. As markets become more diverse and more segmented the statistical problems of research will become correspondingly more difficult.

In the next decade there will be a number of things we can do to overcome these problems. We will need to be much more willing to trust—and use—in-depth qualitative research allied with innovative use of stimulus material. Already qualitative research is extensively used. It is not, however, always regarded as reliable or as valid as quantitative research simply because the sample sizes are too small. But when it comes to undoing the knots that Rod Cameron talks about it may be much more useful. Large quantitative studies are useful for segmentation and confirmation, but to really get into the hearts and souls of Generation MM we need to talk to them in much more meaningful ways.

Companies will also need to jettison much of the research they use to evaluate advertising—recall research, for instance. Recall research, which is designed to measure whether or not people think they have seen an ad, often makes advertising agencies feel good but tells the client little about actual behaviour. The inherent implausibility of such research is indicated by the two terms used to describe its components—aided and unaided recall. What most of it actually measures is whether or not people are too polite to say they haven't actually seen your company's wonderful ad.

We will also have to move from large-scale quantitative studies, which get pictures at particular points of time, towards more continuous tracking methodologies. Already the data that come from supermarkets on stock movements are an indication of what will be possible with better database management and more interactive marketing.

But most importantly—in a knowledge-based and diverse economy—we need to have more faith in creativity and innovation. Research is important. It can help us to avoid mistakes. But to target Generation MM successfully we will need to show the same flexibility and imagination that they will be bringing to their lives.

Brands, identity and corporate values

In the past few years it has finally become clear to everyone that brands have tangible value. In the new millennium we will need to remember that it is *intangibles* that create that value—particularly the values the brand represents.

Marketers have been aware of this for some time, but it came home to the financial community only during the 1980s. During 1988, for instance:

- RJR Nabisco was the centre of a $25 billion takeover fight in which the main prizes were Nabisco biscuits and Winston cigarettes
- Philip Morris bought Kraft for $12.9 billion—four times the value of Kraft's 'tangible' assets
- Nestle paid $4.5 billion—five times book value—to take over Rowntree and gain Kit Kat and other brands

We could say that these takeovers were symptoms of the merger and acquisition boom of the times. This could be partly true. But in every one of the cases the avowed aim of the predators was to gain control of well-known *brands.*

In simple terms, a brand is a name that customers know and react to. In many respects it is an intangible—but like many other intangibles it has a value. The brand influences the buyer's perception of a product and, by doing so, adds value. Water and sugar—for instance—are just commodities. Mix them together with some other things and you get cola. Call the colas Pepsi and Coca-Cola, market and promote them, and you have a brand.

There are, of course, some legal and economic reasons for that being the case. The legal one is a century old—the introduction of trademark law which enabled companies to establish a name as a legally protectable asset. The economic reason is the shift from selling everything from the local store to the mass marketing of goods. In such a situation manufacturers try to give their products a distinctive name. For instance, George Eastman invented a camera. He called it Kodak because it was 'short, vigorous, incapable of being misspelt . . . and meant nothing'.

There are various practical illustrations of the value of brands.

First, in marketing. Honda has built for itself a reputation of quality and performance. In the United States, when Honda launched its lawnmower products it used for its advertising the notion of 'your other Honda'—picturing the lawnmower in a garage. The campaign was very successful because the Honda car image was translated into an image of quality and reliability for the company's other products. These were sold through a cost-effective marketing campaign which built on existing consumer perceptions.

There are some contrary examples, nevertheless. It is difficult, for instance, to imagine Philip Morris going into the pharmaceutical field and piggyback-selling a chest infection cure on the Marlboro name! But, within reason, the principle holds.

A second practical illustration is in terms of costs. About 90 per cent of all new product launches fail. To build a national brand in the United States costs about $60 million, in Japan $30 million and in Britain $20 million. Surveys of consumer goods show that the number one brand in any market earns a 20 per cent return. In contrast, the number two earns around 5 per cent and the rest lose money. Anyone launching a new product needs to take those facts into account and consider whether the risk is worth it or not.

A third practical illustration is in the field of internal motivation. Because a name means a particular thing to consumers, it is possible to motivate company staff to maintain that image.

Since 1988 the quantification of brand values has become much more precise. The United Kingdom Accounting Standards Board has decided that it is legitimate to recognise the value of brands on companies' balance sheets. An international organisation, Interbrand, has begun to value—and rank—brands by looking at the worldwide sale of products carrying the brand name and the brand's operating income. It then assesses the income that would have been generated if the brand was *generic*, and subtracts that amount in order to come up with the *brand* value. On the basis of its calculations Coca-Cola is the most valuable brand at $39 billion, followed by Marlboro $38.7 billion, IBM $17 billion, Motorola $15 billion, Hewlett-Packard $13 billion, Microsoft $11.7 billion, Kodak $11.1 billion, Budweiser $11.3 billion, Kelloggs $11 billion and Nescafe $10.3 billion.

We can see why Sir Hector Laing of United Biscuits once said: 'Buildings age and become dilapidated. Machines wear out. Cars rust. But what lives on are brands'.

Strong brands also attract premium prices from consumers. *The Economist* reported in December 1995 that a motor industry analyst at the Boston Consulting Group had made a fascinating comparison of two cars—the Toyota Corolla and GM's Geo Prizm. In 1989 the Corolla sold for $9000 more than the Geo Prizm, and its secondhand value was 18 per cent higher at the end of 1995. The remarkable thing is that both cars were made by a Toyota/GM joint venture in Fremont, North California. As both cars cost the same to make, the impact of the brand premium on profit was massive.

The United States *Women's Wear Daily*'s Infotrac survey of attitudes found that, while those in the fashion industry distinguish between national and designer brands, private label brands, retail store brands and non-brands, the average consumer sees only two categories—brand and non-brand. More importantly, consumers associate known brands with quality, value and image. Almost 70 per cent of them will pay more for a brand they like.

In the new millennium, when people are searching for certainty and security, this phenomenon is going to be even more important. The strong brand is going to be a guarantee of quality, value and reliability. The alienated member of Generation MM is going to opt for the familiar—the secure—and that is going to be the brand that has been a guide to products that have demonstrated their worth.

But Generation MM is also going to be searching for more than just security and reassurance. It is going to be searching for a brand that represents values as well as value.

The brand will need to personify the corporate values of its owner. It will need to be associated with philanthropy, environmental responsibility and community awareness. In the past few years we have begun to see the impact of boycotts on brands. Exxon has been plagued by fundamentalists who believe the company logo is a satanic symbol. Royal Dutch Shell retreated in the face of a Europe-wide boycott following the allegations of Greenpeace about the Brent Spar oil rig. Nestle is still recovering from the international boycott provoked by a dispute over its activities in marketing formula milk in Third World countries. In Australia in 1995 French restaurants and businesses were forced to erect signs distancing themselves from the French nuclear testing in the Pacific.

If a protester wants to mount a campaign, the simplest way to do so is around a commonly recognised symbol. In most countries during the 1960s and 1970s 'Liberate Zimbabwe' stickers probably appealed only to aficionados of political slogans. But a campaign accusing Nestle of misleading Third World mothers and damaging the health of babies was sure to attract more attention.

In the 21st century one act or problem of one company will be able to be flashed around the world in an instant. The glare of publicity will no longer be in one community but in the global community, even though the conventional media might not at first get to hear about it. This happened with the new Intel chip, whose problems were thoroughly exposed on the Internet before they surfaced in the business media.

Unless companies live their values—and demonstrate the highest standards day in and day out—it will only take a nanosecond for Generation MM to spread the word around the world that they have failed the new millennium's generation. And to demonstrate values companies will also need to demonstrate that they are doing good in the community.

Philanthropy is not about companies feeling good—it's about them actually doing good

There have always been business people happy to provide large philanthropic donations. A few have realised that the donations might help them in seeking mitigation of sentence should their business activities land them in court. Some have sought immortality through foundations named after them or their companies. Some have taken seriously the need for charity.

Equally, there are some economists who argue that the most socially responsible thing a corporation can do is make a profit, return value to its shareholders, and contribute to society in that way.

Each year The Conference Board in the United States surveys some 4000 companies to ascertain trends in corporate giving. The latest survey shows that in 1994 US companies increased their giving by 2.9 per cent after some years of steady or reduced levels of contribution. Education, averaging 35 per cent of corporate giving, was the most supported sector. It was followed by health and human services, which received 25 per cent of donations. Culture and the arts and community groups both received about 11 per cent.

As to who gave what, and how much, the clear leaders were the pharmaceutical and media/publishing industries, which contributed 1.5 per cent of pre-tax income. Close behind them were the energy, mining and paper industries, contributing 1.4 per cent. The chemical industry contributed 1.2 per cent. The lowest ranking donors were utilities—0.6 per cent of pre-tax income.

By way of specific company examples, General Electric gives some $20 million a year to high schools in fourteen cities, Amoco is running a mentoring program for young men on Chicago's West Side and Eastman Kodak contributes about $15 million a year to various company-related purposes. The Kodak Scholars program offers scholarships to more than 100 students at universities that offer technology-transfer studies. The Kodak Learning Challenge program has paid for time off for 700 employees who do mathematics and science teaching in Rochester schools around the Kodak headquarters. And Chrysler runs a childhood literacy program in which some 20 000 employee-volunteers serve as mentors in schools near local Chrysler plants.

Closely allied with straightout philanthropy is 'cause-related' marketing. In this, products and services are sold through joint promotions with charities and other groups.

In June 1995 *Marketing Magazine* reported on the results of a major MORI research project on consumers' attitudes towards cause-related marketing and the companies that use it. The report, released in December 1994, found that:

- 84 per cent of adult Americans believe that cause marketing creates a positive company image
- 66 per cent would switch brands and 62 per cent would switch retailers in order to support a cause they care about
- 54 per cent would pay more for a product in support of a cause, with almost one-quarter saying they would pay up to 10 per cent more
- 78 per cent would be more likely to buy something associated with a cause
- 62 per cent are impressed by a company that commits to a cause for more than one year

Now, as we have seen, people don't always tell market researchers the truth. It is highly possible that consumers say they are concerned about causes because that is what is expected of them—but then behave differently when it comes to the purchase.

What makes the MORI research interesting is that it found there is a population group—about 10 per cent—that is not only the most socially conscious but also acts as opinion leader. People in this group believe very strongly in supporting companies which support causes and are prepared to urge others to do the same. They are also conscious of companies which they associate with what they see as *unacceptable* cause-related practices. A parallel occurred in Australia recently when North Broken Hill—Australia's largest export woodchipping company—sponsored a major exhibition of the famous landscape painter, Arthur Streeton. Both at the launch and in the newspapers afterwards a variety of activists criticised the company for the sponsorship and used it as a lever to attack export woodchipping.

Around the world European, Japanese and Taiwanese companies are adopting cause-related marketing campaigns. A Taiwanese soft-drink maker, for instance, sought to combat Coke and Pepsi by positioning itself as a responsible Chinese company. It sponsored a campaign to help residents of a flood-devastated part of China that had been the ancestral home of many Taiwanese Chinese. The company, King Kar, followed this up by forming a link with a Buddhist nun, Shen Yen. This campaign resulted in 10 per cent of the Taiwanese population making regular donations to Shen Yen's missionary work. In a few years more than $100 million was raised. And in Australia, Pal petfood is associated with helping endangered species through its massive World Animal Day support for the World Wide Fund for Nature.

The emerging difference in philanthropy is that it is more closely linked to corporate and business goals. As cause-related marketing indicates, it is not just about the company feeling good but about the company doing good.

Generation MM will be a generation which values, and searches out, the ethical and the responsible. It will also be a generation with high levels of cynicism—likely to turn against companies whose actions it sees to be hypocritical.

Companies can respond to the demands of Generation

MM primarily by ensuring that they demonstrate their values in everything they do. They can also respond by ensuring that they are seen to be acting responsibly, not only within their own domain but also with the wider range of stakeholders they touch.

Increasingly, this wider aim won't be just about cash. It will also be about the sort of contributions that Kodak and Chrysler are making in providing people to teach in schools. It will be about companies giving executives time off to go and help not-for-profit groups and community organisations with everything from working bees to management and technical experience. It will also be about associating company brands with causes that people care about.

While companies will help others by becoming associated with philanthropy, they will also help themselves. Their involvement in the community, in the arts and with causes will ensure that their managers and staff are exposed to what is going on in the wider world and will sensitise them to the sensitivities of consumers and communities.

Above all else we need to remember that Generation MM won't be satisfied with occasional acts of philanthropy. Instead, it will expect companies to be good citizens all the time. Supporting causes will be just one part of this new level of company responsibility. The other part will be ensuring that the company—and its brands—reflect the total set of corporate values that Generation MM will be seeking in those it deals with.

Not only, however, will it want Corporation MM to demonstrate values—it will want value as well.

Value will be more important than price in consumer choice

The cynics argue that brand loyalty lasts about as long as it takes a competitor to slash prices.

Retailers around the world are suffering from profound changes in shopping patterns as people shop less frequently and search out lower prices. At Christmas over the past few years retailers have been forced to slash prices before Christmas in order to generate trade, and then slash them further to meet the anticipated demand for post-Christmas bargains. Over the past decade declining real wages in much of the Western world have meant that most wage-earning consumers are much more price-conscious.

Yet, while price may be important, value is something else again. A Coopers & Lybrand retail industry survey, reported in *Research Alert* in November 1995, probed what consumers thought constituted value. Some 37 per cent of consumers quoted reasonable price—not just price but reasonable price—as defining value. This was followed by: quality of product, 33 per cent; you get what you pay for, 12 per cent; it's a bargain, 6 per cent; it's a durable product, 5 per cent; all other factors, 7 per cent.

Value also extends to the psychological value a consumer gets from a product or service. As we have seen, consumers will pay a premium for a product—identical in almost every respect to another product—because the brand with which it is labelled is seen to provide value.

Even if we assume that many of the citizens of the 21st century are going to be poor there will still be a role for value. Faced with competing and difficult choices, they may well, though poor, still choose the products which provide them with a sense of belonging to a wider and richer world. That sense of belonging may come from psychological brand value or from a manufactured product of excellence. Whichever, it will be a product that conveys a sense of security, solidity and value. But, as it seems highly probable that the typical global Generation MM member is going to be richer, they will almost certainly be looking for more than their parents' generation was able to achieve. 'More' will not only be *quantitatively* more but also *qualitatively* more—not just more rice and meat but better rice and better meat.

Of course, the quest for more will always be limited by physical realities. You can only have so many goods, so much conspicuous consumption. In the end the real symbol that things are better will be the value of what you possess and of what you aspire to.

7 The culture and organisation of Corporation MM

At business dinners in Anglo-Saxon countries you often get an after-dinner speech about the need for less regulation. Less often do you get oysters. Anglo-Saxons suspect they might be poisoned by them.

The two phenomena, unlikely as it seems, are actually linked.

In a recent book, the noted British economist Robert Neild[29] analyses the respective fortunes of the French and English oyster industry. In the 1850s the English were keen oyster consumers—eating as many as the French. However, the unregulated English industry was destroyed when the oyster beds were overfished and sewage seeped in. Today, English oyster consumption amounts to a few million a year. In France—where the industry has been regulated since the 19th century to avoid overfishing and pollution—consumption is around two billion a year.

Now, as we enter a new millennium, the oyster has a special relevance to the culture and value of the 21st century company—Corporation MM.

First, it shows that regulation can be good for industry and, as a result, ought sometimes to be embraced. That's self-evidently true in areas such as the waste management industry, the growth of which has been driven by increased environmental regulation. But regulation can also be good for industry because it provides a benchmark for the values that Generation MM will be seeking. The English oyster industry was destroyed because the industry destroyed demand. Illness and deaths demonstrated that it was dangerous to eat oysters—that the industry could not be trusted.

Second, it shows that trust and values are crucial factors in corporate success. When trust, values and morality are important we need to look at ways of developing corporate cultures which recognise, reward and internalise them and corporate structures which reflect them and create opportunities for co-operation and dialogue within the company and with Generation MM.

Values, trust, trustworthiness, co-operation and dialogue—how many 20th century companies are actually demonstrating these characteristics to consumers and staff?

'All of us!' is the immediate chorus—from whole choirs of managers who are busily downsizing, re-engineering, diversifying, reorganising and causing upheaval among company staff, communities and even countries. The chorus, unfortunately, is like the performers in a Mozart opera singing a beautiful love duet while plotting to kill the Emperor. The chorus is singing something which is in marked contrast to what's actually happening on stage.

To create companies which genuinely reflect Generation MM values one needs to look at how their culture can drive their performance; at how they can be organised to provide the flexibility needed to meet the diverse needs of uncertain times and diverse markets; at the style by which they need to be managed; and at the ways in which employee trust can be nurtured so as to unleash the productive potential of Generation MM.

Rediscover your company's soul—and profit from it

The great comedian Groucho Marx once said that all you needed to succeed in life was honesty and sincerity. And, he continued, when you learn how to fake them you've got it made!

During the 1980s this philosophy seemed to be one which motivated many businesses. Greed, self-interest and amorality dominated. The decade was marked by anomie—the social phenomenon of the weakening of moral guidelines and the blurring of differences between right and wrong. Ironically, much of the 1980s self-interest was justified by reference to Adam Smith and his historic book *The Wealth of Nations,*[30] even though Adam Smith always saw himself as a philosopher concerned with values and morality, rather than as just an economist.

We now look back on the decade and see the crass materialism and outright dishonesty as the products of a greedy few. Yet, for the public as a whole, the cult of self-interest seemed to permeate all of business and politics. In the 21st century the demand on business will be to demonstrate that it is motivated by community interest rather than the self-interest of a few highly paid managers.

Already, a variety of surveys are indicating the extent of this shift in values.

A United States market research firm, the Walker Group, undertook a survey in which three-quarters of the respondents said they would avoid purchasing from companies with a bad image. Some 47 per cent said that if all other product and price attributes were equal they would buy from the company that they believed to be more socially responsible. Another research company, Frankel & Co., polled 682 primary grocery shoppers; 69 per cent of them reported purchasing certain brands primarily because of their link to a worthy cause.

PR Reporter, a New Hampshire-based journal which reports on communication and social trends, discussed in an October 1995 issue a survey undertaken by the communication company Porter/Novelli. The survey involved two parallel lines of research in which 2645 customers were asked to rate various factors that influenced their buying decisions, while 279 corporate public relations executives were asked how they felt consumers would respond.

Naturally, both groups named product quality as one of the most important factors in a consumer's buying decision, although only 78 per cent of consumers ranked it thus compared with 87 per cent of executives. The clear implication is that, while consumers strongly focus on product quality, it is still not as significant in their minds as it is in the minds of company executives.

The second most important factor was how a company handles consumer complaints and problems. Again there was a difference between consumer and company. Sixty per cent of consumers ranked it as important compared with 54 per cent of company executives.

The next most important factors were:

- fairness and equality in hiring, with the issue being important to 24 per cent of consumers and only 4 per cent of executives
- record on environmental issues—consumers 20 per cent versus executives 4 per cent
- employing people in the consumer's neighbourhood—20 per cent versus 3 per cent
- record of workers' safety—16 per cent versus 1 percent

When we look at the survey we see two striking things. After product quality all the important issues in the consumers' minds are to do with how companies behave. Yet these same behavioural issues are not considered very important by the executives given the responsibility for shaping the company image.

When consumers were asked to rank the five major influences on their buying habits they picked: product quality; method of handling complaints; the way a company handles a crisis in which it is at fault; accusations by government agencies about product safety; and accusations of illegal or unethical trading practices.

Significantly, boycotts by animal rights activists and openness in dealing with the media were among the three least important issues—except among younger people, Generation MM, for whom the most important factors were animal rights boycotts and challenges by either consumer or government groups about product safety. Equally significantly, women were most influenced by issues to do with bias against women, fairness and equality in hiring, and occupational health and safety record.

The survey makes it abundantly clear that behaviour and

values influence consumer attitudes and that they are likely to be even more influential with the next generation.

A number of organisations are responding to this shift already. A Harvard Business School academic, Joseph Badarracco Jnr, has brought together 47 case studies on business ethics in his work[31]. The bulk of the book is devoted to what Badarracco calls 'ethical responsibilities in co-operative capitalism'. He points out that corporate social responsibility blurs company boundaries and creates complex links between firms and other organisations and stakeholders. The Institute of Public Relations—the United Kingdom's professional association for public relations executives—has recently changed its definition of public relations so as to take the new reality of reputation management into account. Now, it says, 'PR practice is the discipline which looks after reputation'.

Lois Hogan, a senior counsellor with the United States firm Jackson, Jackson & Wagner, has been doing doctoral research on values and their role in organisational culture and employee relations. Some of her work has been included in a new book *Rediscovering the Soul of Business: A Renaissance of Values.*[32] 'There is a huge interest in this topic—a hunger for wholeness that is palpable. Now we need visionaries who can translate this into practical ways that will affect our practice.' Hogan is not frightened to use the word 'soul' when talking about business and says that putting soul back into business pays off in the bottom line. She says that the area is still unmapped territory and that the answers probably cannot be made into programmatic models.

Hogan specifies two areas where action can be taken. Business needs to provide time for reflection: 'We move so fast we totally forget about the role renewal plays in the cycle of life'. Second, there has to be a role for beauty, art and grace: 'Business has become so functional it doesn't often provide these, or they are the first things cut'. She adds: 'A "soulful" way of working would be to look at ways to integrate these things so an employee's life could be fuller and richer, so they couldn't feel fragmented'.

Perhaps the best example of how this new concern with values can be put into practice is the ice-cream company, Ben & Jerry's. The company donates 7 per cent of its pre-tax profits to a foundation for distribution to charities. It seeks suppliers and outlets among farmers in developing countries and at-risk youth in American cities and it seeks to make its 'social balance sheet' as impressive as its financial balance sheet (it actually publishes a social balance sheet alongside its financial data in its annual report). Its founders—Ben Cohen and Jerry Greenfield—say that business, as the most powerful force in society, must be committed to serving the common good.

It is significant that Cohen and Greenfield describe themselves as 'hippies' who have made money out of what were 1960s values.

The point about these 1960s 'hippy' values is that they were not actually the values of the sixties but the values of the baby-boomers coming of age during the period. The 1960s values were predominantly disapproval of pre-marital sex, censorship and conformity—the things against which many of the young were reacting.

Today, when we see concern for the environment, more relaxed lifestyles and changes in language and values, we can see their roots in those halcyon days. If you look around a room of middle-aged managers today you can look beyond their blue or grey suits and know that not so long ago they too wore flares, safari suits and body-tight paisley shirts and had flowers in their hair. Many of them may have heard more about sex, drugs and rock and roll than they were actually involved in, but nevertheless they were profoundly influenced by their 1960s experiences.

The language of companies today is often the language of the 1960s—values, reinvention, empowerment, commitment, devolution, consumer sovereignty, responsibility and so on. The 1960s were a generation which believed that the world could be revolutionised and reinvented. That dream has now become an everyday reality, with consequences for us all.

And when we look at our own lives it is easy to understand why we and Generation MM are so concerned about values.

We have lived through the 1980s. We don't approve of dishonesty. We want people to recognise our integrity. We try to do the right thing by people. We give to charity to help address problems. We are concerned about drug-taking and violence. And we want to be sure that we can trust the institutions and organisations with which we deal.

It is a simple step for managers to step outside their company and judge it by the values and standards by which they themselves think the world should operate. If you do, and if your company fails the test, it may well be going to fail the test of the 21st century—in terms of both morality and profit. For in the millennium, as we will see, altruism is good business.

Altruism is good business—so live ethical values

In the United States there are a number of investment funds which describe themselves as 'ethical' funds. This does not mean that they think they are more ethical than their competitors. Instead it seeks to convey the flavour of their investment policies. Some of them focus on investments in companies with good environmental records. During the 1970s and 1980s they were the first funds to divest themselves of investments in companies operating in South Africa. They were suspicious of companies which were involved in countries with poor human rights records. And they were prepared to use their financial muscle to force companies to act ethically. The massive Californian government employees' fund—Calpers—has been a leading exponent of shareholder activism designed to pressure boards of directors to adopt high moral standards on issues as diverse as equal opportunity and occupational health and safety.

During the period in which these investment funds were emerging, the financial news was dominated by the freewheeling activities of the 1980s entrepreneurs—the Gordon Gekkos of the United States and the Alan Bonds and Christopher Skases of Australia. Lloyd's of London was travelling the world encouraging the citizens of former colonies—from South

Africa and Australia to Canada and the United States—to become a part of the old boys' club.

In retrospect, it is easy to guess which investor category performed best. But at the time it would have been a brave person who predicted that the ethical funds would beat the stockmarket index. In fact they did. Most other companies grouped under the ethical banner also consistently outperformed the rest of the market.

A number of conclusions can be drawn from this.

First, the short-term, 'get rich quick' financial engineering of some entrepreneurs was as doomed to ultimate failure as all the previous booms had been. From the Dutch tulip boom to the South Seas Bubble to the roaring twenties to the greedy eighties, booms have inevitably been followed by bust and the geniuses of the day have been shown to be without substance.

Second, the companies that build long-term value tend to be the companies not obsessed by self-interest but concerned about their role in wider society. These altruistic companies are the companies that balance the interests of all their stakeholders, and see profit as a result of a company's total goals rather than an end in itself.

Third, the companies which survive the periodic bouts of insanity that infect markets are usually the companies with solid values that inoculate them from the speculative disease.

So, how can we absorb and build on the values that inoculate us against the fever?

We have already discussed some of them—commitment to ethical behaviour, acceptance of corporate responsibility and so on—and we have noted the emerging tendency to judge companies by the ethical standards of individuals. And it is this last—the process of judging by individual standards—which encourages us to learn to live by the ethical values that create the altruism that will contribute to business success.

A few examples illustrate the point. First, when living by ethical standards we show that we respect other individuals. The law may outlaw sexual harassment or discrimination, but it is not the law that makes an ethical person treat others with respect. It is an awareness that certain standards of behaviour are unacceptable.

Second, we need to be open in communications. The people who play office politics, plot, conspire or complain secretly about others are all, in fact, undermining the ethical standards of the business. Open communication allows problems to be confronted and dealt with. Secrecy allows them to fester and to institutionalise dishonesty and lack of integrity.

Third, we need to be altruistic about the resources available within the company. All companies need today to strive to do more with fewer resources. The best outcome for the company is to co-operatively allocate the resources to the optimum use. The worst outcome is for individuals to hoard resources, or to manoeuvre to acquire them for self-aggrandisement.

The three examples are so simple as to be almost banal. Yet day in and day out we see people in organisations doing the opposite of what we know to be acceptable, and intelligent, standards of behaviour.

Business ethics are about good business. There is nothing complex about them. It all gets down to doing the right thing. The vast majority of people know that there is a difference between right and wrong. They have an internal alarm which gears up as they get close to the line between the two, and which rings when the line is crossed. In most cases ethical behaviour is simply a matter of listening to the internal alarm. And in most cases ethical corporate cultures are simply cultures that ensure that people are not pressured into ignoring the alarm when it rings.

One test as to whether your corporate culture has successfully absorbed these values lies in how you treat someone who actually rings the alarm for you.

Whistleblowers will become heroes, not heretics

There are always huge social pressures to conform—and to avoid whistleblowing—from our first days at school to the end of our working careers. We've all been in a schoolroom where the whole class has been kept in because no one will own up and no one will point the finger at the guilty party. The Al Pacino film *Scent of a Woman* recounts how a blind man sees the dilemmas this can cause and finds a way through it. In the film the characters question what is the right, moral, brave course—maintain silence or be honest—in the face of conflicting codes.

Everyone has known somebody who has drawn attention to an irregularity and has been depicted as a zealot or a troublemaker, and made into a pariah as a result.

In Australia there is even a derogatory term to describe whistleblowing—dobbing in. 'You wouldn't be a dobber, would you?' is a question often heard in school playgrounds.

The Economist of 19 August 1995 looked at the contrast between enthusiasm for business ethics and the treatment of whistleblowers. It gave two poignant examples. In the first, a General Electric engineer helped the United States Justice Department take legal action against the company for allegedly inadequately testing a jet engine sold to the Defence Department. The company settled out of court, and says extensive testing has proven the engines to be safe. The engineer has left GE, branded a troublemaker. In the second case, two engineers warned of the problems that ultimately led to the Challenger space shuttle disaster in 1986. Nobody heeded the warnings and seven people died. Although United States law prohibits action against whistleblowers for raising a concern, the two engineers' careers suffered.

The problem the whistleblower confronts is the conflict between the pressure to conform and the need for organisations to ensure that their behaviour is acceptable and ethical. This problem even confronts organisations which themselves encourage whistleblowing. Two such groups have suffered as a result of not having a whistleblower within their own ranks.

The Body Shop cosmetics chain, for instance, built its empire on ethical behaviour and concern for the environment. The CEO, Anita Roddick, was prominent in many international environmental campaigns. Yet The Body Shop was forced to rephrase advertising claims that said that its products were not tested on animals.

The pre-eminent international whistleblower is the Greenpeace environmental organisation. Greenpeace's own performance, in ethical terms, has at times been abysmal. In the case of the battle with Shell over the Brent Spar oil rig, a series of oceanographers had insisted that the deepsea disposal option was the safest. Greenpeace, on the basis of some hasty dippings in the Spar's tanks, 'refuted the claim'. Aided by a compliant media, which used Greenpeace's own video release and pretended that it was news footage independently gathered, Greenpeace won the public case. Greenpeace was wrong and almost certainly knew it was wrong, but no one blew the whistle.

It is easy to highlight the hypocrisy of such organisations. What is more important is to work out what to do about whistleblowers.

The Economist reports that Dun & Bradstreet, TRW (a defence supplier) and General Dynamics have all appointed internal ethics officers or ombudsmen to help protect ethical values.

More and more companies are instituting ethical codes which spell out the standards of behaviour the company wants to achieve. But even these can be difficult. In some developing countries bribery is more akin to a user-pays system than to corruption. The government doesn't pay its officials—or, if it does, it pays them in currency whose value has been reduced by rampant inflation. The officials then impose agreed 'fees' for various services such as issuing a visa or allowing goods through customs. If you don't pay the fee you don't get the visa, or your goods rot away on the wharfs or at the airfield. The *ethical* answer is that you don't pay bribes. The *pragmatic* answer is that it is impossible to do business in such a country unless you do. The big problem arises when the small fee for service becomes a request for a major payment—an unethical payment. As with all sins and lies, how do you draw the line? Many companies draw the veil rather than the line and just pretend it isn't happening. Such an attitude obviously undermines the internal credibility of any ethical code.

But perhaps the best code is the one which ensures that the whistleblower in any situation is the company CEO.

In simple terms that means that the company should have systems which identify problems as they arise and that the company itself should be the organisation which goes public with the information, rather than waiting for it to emerge later. When Johnson & Johnson was hit by the Tylenol problem the company did the ethical thing. It went out and told consumers of the risk, and recalled the affected products. As a result its corporate reputation was enhanced.

The public and the media accept that people make mistakes. They don't, however, accept coverups. Most of the crises occur not because companies did wrong but because they didn't own up, and got caught. When they cover things up they expose themselves to the accusation that they have betrayed their own values and ethics, and thus they normally prolong and widen the media coverage of any incident.

But when the CEO is the whistleblower he or she can become the hero rather than the heretic—and demonstrate that the company is serious about its values. And the CEO who is serious about values will be a CEO who understands why Generation MM may not accept that every company will automatically be moral and responsible.

Embracing regulation *loosens* the regulatory bonds

Most business people, thinking about the social changes coming with the new millennium, will have already begun to develop a suspicion that one thing won't change . . . regulation. If we think about the emphasis on values, the importance of the environment and the demands of diversity discussed later—let alone the millenarian hopes—it is obvious that people are going to want to control business more tightly. The fear of business will be: what about our freedom to do business?

In the new millennium, though, freedom will come within a framework in which rights and obligations are balanced. No one today would argue that business has the right to pollute the atmosphere. No one would argue that business has the right to sell shoddy products which maim or kill people. *No one* is free to do whatever they like.

The reality is that the social and political changes will lead to greater demands for regulation. That regulation will fall most heavily on those who argue for 'freedom' and 'rights' and who try to resist the changes. At an advertising industry forum in 1995, at which I advanced this view, a questioner from the floor argued that we must always resist regulation because otherwise you could end up like the tobacco industry. I replied that the tobacco industry had actually been remarkably successful. They had a product that killed people—directly or indirectly through smoking or passive smoking—which they had managed to keep on the market in the developed world to the extent that they still had 25 per cent of consumers using the product. While fighting a rearguard action in the developed world, they were expanding rapidly into the Third World.

The decision to put warnings on packaging freed the companies—for a while—from some legal challenges, indicating the advantage of active rather than defensive responses to regulation.

But the tobacco industry is probably not a precedent for anything in the regulatory field; it will be the case that regulation will fall most lightly on those who understand that rights and obligations must be balanced and who become involved in dialogue with their opponents and their regulators. It will fall most lightly on those who see the first puffs of smoke from a fire and douse them before they become an all-consuming conflagration. And it will fall most lightly on those companies that anticipate community demands and deal with the issues actively rather than defensively.

It will do so because—while Generation MM will make new demands—Generation MM will also be a generation racked by fear and uncertainty. Companies reaching out to them, and reassuring them, will be more likely to succeed than those confronting them, adding to their anxiety and alienation and provoking yet more demands for regulation. And those that embrace regulation will also be sending a powerful message to Generation MM—that values are important to the companies as well.

These companies will also send powerful messages through the language they use about their business; the role their CEO takes; and the structures they adopt.

The world is not a zero-sum game and the days of victory metaphors are dead

To read much management literature, or to listen to many managers talk at work, is to imagine that managers spend half their time preparing for combat.

Two of the most popular marketing writers in the world—Al Ries and Jack Trout—were photographed for the front cover of one of their books[33] clad in military garb, atop a tank. Inside the book the military analogies proliferate. *The Art of War* by Sun-Tsze,[34] a Chinese philosopher, was a management bestseller in the late 1980s. And in one of the most tasteless pieces of management writing imaginable, one author has talked about how Hitler's military oratory can be used as the basis for motivation.

Battlefield language is often heard on the playing field as well, although business also adds to its store of victory metaphors from more traditional sporting analogies. Players have to get on the team, someone has to kick a goal and there's no value in coming second.

The superficial rationale for such language is that it reflects the fact that business is supposed to be about winning and losing—winning and losing market share or winning or losing advantage. We are told time and time again that, because the fundamental feature of business is competition, there must be winners and losers.

In very simple terms this is undoubtedly true. Some companies do win market share from others. Some individuals do win promotion and others lose their jobs. Some companies are seen as winners and others as losers. In some areas of human activity—sport, some professions and the entertainment business—economists do recognise a 'winner take all' phenomenon where the market leaders get grossly disproportionate incomes compared with the other players. The 'winners' in these fields are really like the triumphant generals of Roman times who attracted the plaudits and the benefits.

But most of the talk about winning and losing assumes that we operate in a zero sum game—in an environment in which we compete over various shares of the cake. If we don't get some of the cake right now we have no other opportunity, because it has all gone.

The reality is that in the 20th century the cake has been getting bigger and bigger all the time. Between 1977 and 1994 the United States' gross domestic product grew by 241 per cent. Japan's GDP grew by 565 per cent, South Korea's by 917 per cent, Singapore's by 819 per cent and Taiwan's by 961 per cent. World GDP doubled between 1970 and 1993. Total world exports increased 15 times. Electricity production almost trebled. Automobile production increased by more than 50 per cent and rice production almost doubled. World GDP in 1993 was estimated at 29.1 trillion US dollars compared with 14.3 trillion in 1970.

More cars, more clothing, more soap bars, more electric power—more products for consumers.

These staggering increases point to a fundamental fact about our society and our globe. Despite continuing poverty the world is generally getting richer and standards of living are increasing. This change is constantly creating new opportunities to grow markets for old products and to supply new needs with new products and services. If we focus just on winning and losing—on whether we do a bit better than the competitor—it is easy to overlook the fact that growing the market is often the real key to success.

Why don't we change our focus?

The first reason is a biological one. Testosterone. The majority of managers are men, and men are afflicted with a biological curse—testosterone. It makes them want to prove that they are bigger, stronger and more successful than other men. In Neolithic times this was a real advantage. It allowed men to get the best game when hunting and choose the most desirable breeding partners. In the 20th century it just tends to make them look foolish.

Second, men tend to participate in more contact sports at schools. Contact sports require controlled aggression. They also foster male bonding which spills over from the playing field to the board room. Any visitor to a money market dealing room will see the after-effects of this bonding vividly displayed.

Third, war has been an overwhelming reality throughout the 20th century. The Russo–Japanese war was followed by World War I which was followed by the Sino–Japanese war which was followed by World War II and then the Korean War and Vietnam. In between, various civil wars, police actions and guerrilla outbreaks have kept the world more at war than at peace.

Even those who have experienced mainly peace in the past 50 years have been constantly exposed to the images and language of war. Where those images and language have related to camaraderie and sacrifice they may well have been positive. But where they have been plain militarism they have scarred our attitudes to life. And today we sit in comfortable chairs in air-conditioned offices looking out over peaceful streets and parks . . . and speculate on how we can kill the opposition!

Meanwhile those who shift their speculations from the narrow focus of military and sporting glory see a different world in which there are millions of new consumers craving for a better life and in which new markets can be enhanced and developed rather than conquered. These managers will also see that the world is more complex than it appears and that shedding the hubris which accompanies the victory metaphors is a step towards understanding how the world really works.

Chaos rules, OK

We like to believe that the very foundation of business is rationality—rational planning, rational organisation, rational decision-making and rational outcomes.

The great inventor and business pioneer Thomas Edison once claimed: 'I never did anything by accident, nor did any of my inventions come indirectly through accident'. And a business writer, Napoleon Hill, spoke of an age of organised effort: 'On every hand we see evidence that organisation is the basis of all financial success'.

Much of 20th century business practice has been directed towards planning and control. The modern automotive industry was built on the assembly line. Under the management system known as Taylorism, business spent much of the 1930s trying to pull apart every human task, measure how long it took and then devise systems to make individuals efficient cogs in the assembly line.

In recent years we have seen business embrace, and then reject, a series of concepts designed to increase control and hence better equip companies to succeed. Some elements of the total quality movement became a sort of cross between Taylorism and evangelical passion. All processes were measured and continuous improvement was plotted and maintained. Re-engineering stripped out layers of management and rendered hundreds of thousands of workers redundant.

On a day-to-day level, companies spend significant amounts of time each year preparing and refining corporate and business plans. Many businesses seek to take uncertainty into account, with contingency planning and commitments to flexibility.

Planning and control has delivered massive benefits in terms of helping to achieve an agreed corporate focus, tightening financial accountability and improving inventory control. Without it most businesses would be doomed. But while the benefits are obvious, so are the failures which stem from apparently rational confidence that we can predict and control the future.

The causes of failure are fourfold. First, too many companies simply don't understand that they operate in a chaotic environment. Second, they make conscious assumptions about the business, its market or its operating environment which are unjustified or plain wrong. Third, they make unconscious—and again erroneous—assumptions about the society in which they operate. Fourth, they create cultures which encourage management hubris.

Newspapers, books and magazines are full of information about the first reason for failure, chaos. While the mathematical concept of chaos is not new, it has proved to be a powerful tool in understanding fields as diverse as the weather, air-conditioning systems and epidemiology. Perhaps most importantly, it is a concept which connects with late 20th century feelings about our age and the uncertainties associated with it. To people who have only the barest understanding of what the concept means, it appears to provide a description of the constant change occurring around them.

Chaos theory is best summarised by the French mathematician Poincaré's statement: 'A very small case, which escapes us, determines a considerable effect which we cannot ignore, and then we say that this effect is due to chance'. In essence, the theory says that very small events can have massive outcomes in complex systems. The most famous illustration of the theory is the assertion that it is theoretically possible for a butterfly flapping its wings on one side of the earth to cause a hurricane on the other.

The theory, significantly, applies to all complex systems (not just physical ones), such as human societies, economies and markets. It is this that makes it so difficult to predict the future—that the environment in which business operates is such that unintended consequences of our actions can be profound. It is why most economists have an appalling track record in forecasting movements in basic economic indicators; why most simple all-encompassing theories—whether they be TQM, re-engineering or some management fad—tend not to produce the predicted results; and why companies who believe their systems are fail-safe end up experiencing disasters.

Once we understand that we operate in a chaotic environment we understand the need for greater flexibility and we understand why we must always be ready for change and surprise. Most importantly, we can understand why planning systems which depend on forecasts and budgets that project the current business into the future so often fail.

The second reason why planning fails relates to our conscious assumptions. We make a perfectly logical and reasonable assumption, then another one, and then another one and finally we have a coherent plan which seems robust—but in fact rests on a series of untested hypotheses.

Even the very best companies occasionally make mistakes because of their conscious assumptions. In the July–August 1995 *Harvard Business Review*, Rita Gunther McGrath and Ian C. Macmillan (from Columbia University and the Wharton School of Finance, respectively) analysed what went wrong at Disney Europe. The Walt Disney Company went into the European theme park business in 1992 and by 1994 had lost more than $1 billion, despite the fact that the Disney park was attracting one million visitors a month, making it Europe's most popular paid tourist destination.

McGrath and Macmillan outline the incorrect assumptions made by Disney:

- The admission price was based on the levels that Japanese and United States Disney theme parks had achieved *gradually*. It was set at a level which failed to take into account the French recession and the determination of the French government to keep the franc's value high.
- Disney assumed that people would stay an average of four days in the park's five hotels. In fact the average stay was two days. The reason—Disney Europe had 15 rides compared with 45 at Disney World. It was possible to experience all 15 rides in one day.
- Euro Disney restaurants were designed on the same basis as those in the United States and Japan as it was anticipated that visitors would 'graze' all day. Instead, patrons followed the European custom of sitting down to dine at lunchtime. They found the restaurants overcrowded and left the park to eat elsewhere.

A chain of assumptions turned out to be faulty when the plan treated the assumptions as facts.

The third reason for planning failures relates to the *unconscious* assumptions that businesses make. The most basic of these assumptions is that the company is the repository of all knowledge and that the rest of the world thinks in the same way that the managers of the company do. Everyone knows an anecdote about how companies make mistakes in moving into markets in other countries and failing to understand the cultural differences involved. For each of these very obvious disasters there are equivalent disasters in domestic markets.

Basically, the problem with unconscious assumptions rests in the failure to recognise that the world is more diverse, more uncertain and less rational than a company clique of like-minded managers can imagine.

The fourth reason for mistakes is the culture that is created in many organisations—a culture which encourages undue deference to senior management. Senior managers are paid large sums to make decisions and provide leadership. Their views on everything from the marketplace to the latest government policy initiative are given prominence in the media. Their perks of office often inspire awe. Inevitably, many of them come to be treated with astonishing deference. Their subordinates don't disagree or, if they do, only very politely. And their head office tends to revolve around them.

Some time ago I was lunching with the CEO of a large company. He arrived a little late because his office had been thrown into minor turmoil when he had simply announced he was going out without saying exactly where. He was a cultured, intelligent man who would never be guilty of arrogance or of imagining that his position gave him any special standing that warranted reverence.

We analysed the incident and decided that head offices had a tendency to function very similarly to medieval royal courts. In such courts the monarch—or CEO—was the centre of power. The courtiers—advisers and head office staff—defined their power and standing in terms of their proximity to the monarch and their knowledge of his or her thoughts and activities. The main characteristics of such courts were deference to the point of reverence and an overriding sense of unreality, which are not conducive to experiment or intellectual challenge, but are conducive to mistakes.

The most common symptom of companies allowing their head office to become like a medieval court is middle managers seeking to win arguments by reference to what they claim the CEO wants or thinks. And companies which operate in such a way persist in making mistakes because they make untested assumptions or accept as facts the opinions of the CEO. Like World War I generals they keep sending the troops over the top and the troops keep getting gunned down.

Avoiding these mistakes is made doubly difficult in a millenarian age when chaos, irrationality and uncertainty are the norm rather than the unusual. To succeed in such an irrational environment, business must be rational about irrationality. It is does not itself have to become irrational, but it does need to learn the limits of rationality and the need for flexible responses to change, surprise and the irrational.

Such flexibility can be encouraged by encouraging diversity within business—by employing people who are keen to challenge the assumptions the company has always made.

Prizing diversity and eccentricity to create competitive advantage

In the 1950s William H. Whyte Jnr coined the term 'organisation man' to describe the typical white collar worker—predictable, controllable and lacking in initiative and individuality. The organisation man had a number of characteristics. For a start, he was a he. He was also white, quintessentially American and pretty much middle class.

Today, with the 21st century approaching, the organisation

man would probably find himself very lost, both in successful companies and in the world as a whole. His world has changed. In the United States one in 14 residents is an immigrant and in the 21st century White Anglo-Saxon Protestants will before long be just another minority, with the population majority comprising Asians, Africans, Hispanics and other hyphenated Americans. Elsewhere, Australia is now one of the world's most successful multicultural societies. Canada—despite the ongoing debate about its future—is a mosaic of cultures in which one in six of the population is an immigrant.

The workforce is reflecting this diversity. In their book, *American Mosaic*,[35] Anthony Carnevale and Susan Stone reveal that the United States workforce is becoming increasingly diverse. In 1990 white men represented 43.1 per cent of the workforce. By 2005, it is estimated, the percentage will have dropped to 38.2 per cent. Over the same period the number of Hispanic women in the workforce is expected to increase from 3.1 per cent to 4.6 per cent. Other ethnic and gender groups show similar movements. The point is that—gradually—the workforce is becoming different and more diverse.

Companies themselves are also reflecting the diversity. More and more of them genuinely operate as transnationals with multinational workforces. ABB (Asea Brown Bouveri), the electrical engineering company, is regarded by many as Europe's most respected company. Its CEO, Percy Barnevik, sees its success as vitally linked to its faith in multiculturalism. The company headquarters staff comprises 171 people from 19 different countries. The official company language is English although only a third of the ABB staff have English as a first language. This means, of course, that at the very least two-thirds of the staff are bilingual.

Indeed, Barnevik could be said to have created the company of the 21st century—the company he describes as 'the multicultural multinational'. Creating such companies, however, requires an approach which encourages tolerance and respect.

In contrast, much US effort to create diversity has seemed to be an end in itself rather than a means of creating more successful companies. In the United States much of the focus on diversity has in fact been a debate about rights, entitlements and quotas in the broader US society.

Diversity quotas have been used as a coded means of activating racial issues to shift blue collar voters from the Democratic Party camp into the Republican camp and managers have been more conscious of the debate about quotas than the business outcomes diversity can provide.

A few examples from recent US management literature on diversity illustrate this tendency. In the September 1994 *Personnel Journal* Shari Caudron reviewed the efforts of various United States companies to develop training in diversity issues. She says that much of the work was still focused on the processes of coming to terms with diversity and sensitising employees to differences in others. In the best companies these processes have been absorbed into the more general effort to develop co-operative teams. However, most companies still tended to see the recognition of diversity as an end in itself, rather than a means to an end. An example of this focus on *process* is given in *PR Reporter* 6 February 1995 by Tracy Gray, strategic partner of a consulting firm, Brown-Olmstead Associates in Atlanta. Gray described their approach to diversity as one which 'includes a synthesis of affirmative action, multiculturalism, valuing differences and quality management of diversity—from which is created a high-performance diversity process'!

Very few companies have taken the next step from process to external outcome. One that has is IDS Financial Services, whose Vice President, Diversity, Richard S. Gaskins, aptly says: 'Our vision of diversity is when leadership and teamwork combine to create an environment through which people's differences can be used to meet the company's goals of people, service, and profitability'.

A former Australian Government Industry and Technology Minister, John Button, has talked about how slow Australia has been to realise the advantage that multiculturalism provides Australian companies. Multiculturalism means that companies have staff skilled in the language, and aware of the culture, of the export markets that the companies need to develop. It means there is experience inside each such company that helps it to operate with diverse cultures; in other words, there are staff whose horizons are wider than those of traditional Australia.

While this political—and academic—debate has proceeded the world has been changing. It is more diverse and that makes markets more diverse. That means that companies which want to succeed in those markets must understand that diversity. We must never forget that the real need for diversity within the company stems from the reality of the marketplace. Day after day we tell each other that companies must strive to be closer to customers and more responsive to their needs. To do that it is essential to understand the customer, who is less and less likely to look much like the image in your morning mirror.

Getting your managers to match Generation MM's outlook is, therefore, a crucial step in winning competitive advantage. That almost certainly means tolerating much more diversity—and even eccentricity—among managers.

In 1980 the oil billionaire Bunker Hunt, in conjunction with members of the Saudi Arabian royal family, set out to corner the silver market. Hunt was a genuine eccentric whose political and economic views were odd, to say the least. Hunt learnt that, in today's world, markets can't be cornered, simply because there are too many players and too many ways in which another commodity can be substituted for whatever commodity you seek to control. While Hunt was unsuccessful in cornering the silver market, he was successful in articulating an important business principle. Asked how much money he had, he said he didn't know. Asked why not, he said: 'Money's not important—it's just how you keep score'.

Hunt may not be the best example of the benefits of eccentricity, but his comment does raise an important insight into success in the 21st century.

We have talked about the need for focus and the need for vision. But the real question is what we actually focus on.

Many people dream of becoming rich. Other than those who have been wise enough to choose wealthy parents, most people don't achieve it—spending their time buying lottery tickets and dreaming. The few that do achieve wealth are normally those who focus not on the money but on the 'how'—on the thing they are doing. The better they do it, the harder they work, the more they learn and improve—the more successful they are.

Companies need managers who think in exactly the same way. Managers who concentrate on making a profit are easy to find. Managers who focus on new profitable ways of doing things are rarer. Managers who concentrate on money—including their own remuneration—frequently abandon ship to seek better paying jobs elsewhere. But managers who focus on achieving excellence can make themselves and their companies more successful.

The first type are the managers that the younger generation—Generation MM—has dubbed 'suits'. The term is meant to be contemptuous and to convey more than mode of dress. The phrase originated in pop culture. Rock bands called the accountants, managers and record company bosses the 'suits', to contrast them with the attitudes and dress of the rock stars themselves.

The second type are the managers who were involved in Silicon Valley start-up companies and who revolutionised the world. In the July–August 1995 *Harvard Business Review,* Harold J. Leavitt of the Stanford Graduate School of Business and Jean Lipman-Blumen of the Claremont Graduate School referred to 'hot groups' operating in Bell Telephone Laboratories:

> The highest status in the organisation went to the people in basic research, the ones doing the most far out, and in the short run, the most impractical work. In many other companies those people would have been pilloried as nerds and long-hairs irrelevant to the real power structure of the organisation.

The problem is that in a millenarian age the unthinkable is very possibly just the sort of thing that is most likely to happen. Safe, secure, narrowly focused managers who seek to conform at all costs are not going to succeed in such an environment. They will see the change around them as a source of fear rather than of opportunity.

The safe, secure manager is essentially an administrator—while the exceptional manager is an opportunistic, flexible, entrepreneurial, risk-taking, boat-rocking, issue-anticipating source of fresh and disturbing ideas.

The safe, secure manager was surprised by the emergence of the 1980s environmental tidal wave and when it arrived was confident that it would go away. The exceptional manager had remembered, or learnt from, the 1960s and realised that a new generation of young people had new concerns about the environment.

The safe, secure manager refers to precedent and tradition—the way things have been done in the past. The exceptional manager asks the most powerful management question of all: 'Why?'. An illustration of the power of this question is given in the film *Starman.* The film's plot revolves around a man from outer space coming to Earth and living among earthlings. Nothing very unusual about the plot, you might think. It gets interesting, though, when the man from outer space goes into a diner with a woman who has befriended him. They start to eat their meal, which is arranged—as it is in diners—with salad, main course and dessert all on the one tray. He starts to eat his dessert first. She says he shouldn't—and that you should eat the dessert last. He looks up and asks the question: 'Why?'.

Many of our practices are like that. We eat our dessert last because that's the way we have always done it. We need to ask why in order to test whether the traditional assumption is right.

In an ever-changing world the person who appears to be eccentric may well be the person who understands best what is going on out there. The person who defends the traditional may understand it least.

The suits will continue to have an important role to play. Keeping score with the money—as Bunker Hunt found—is still necessary, after all. But, increasingly, working out how it can be made will require the imagination and creativity that come with an iconoclastic—even eccentric—approach to life.

Creating corporate cultures which encourage imagination and creativity must start with the creation of cultures which encourage staff to learn, grow and use their intelligence.

Creating a learning culture

The industrial relations system in Australia provides a framework within which employers and employees can reach what are called enterprise agreements. The agreements cover everything from pay rates to work practices. Over the past decade they have been one of the most important ways in which Australian companies have become more competitive and workers have been persuaded to accept change.

In 1995 Australia's major brewing company—Carlton & United Breweries (CUB)—reached an agreement with the workers at its Kent Brewery in Sydney. In the agreement CUB and the unions declared that the survival of the enterprise meant it must change at a rate at least equal to that of its competitors.

How was the change to be achieved? The enterprise agreement noted that all change is accompanied by learning and that 'a learning enterprise is one where individuals, teams and the enterprise are continually learning and sharing in the development, transfer and use of knowledge and skills to produce continual improvement and the creation of a dynamic competitive advantage'.

Peter Roberts, writing about the agreement in the *Australian Financial Review* of 13 September 1995, said: 'Communicating, responsiveness and flexibility is really about faster learning . . . not old-style training which is about someone being in control of knowledge and delivering it to others. Learning is about getting people together to find every possible way in which they can be developed'.

The CUB agreement epitomises an attitudinal change which is occurring across the world—an attitudinal change which must transform how companies operate and how managers manage.

In the 19th century most companies made things and success came to those whose manufacturing was the most efficient. The employees' role was to service the machines and implement the instructions issued by managers. In the new millennium most companies know things, and success comes to those who harness that knowledge to create a market advantage.

With rapidly declining product cycles and cheap and freely available technology, the chances of maintaining competitive advantage simply on the basis of the excellence of a company's equipment are slim. The real source of competitive advantage comes from how clever companies—and the people within them—are.

The Economist of 28 October 1995 reported on how United States companies are beginning to create inhouse universities. While cynics might claim that inhouse education is essential to redress the failures of the United States education system, the real reason is different. *The Economist* said:

> American companies seem to have learnt three basic rules about the modern workplace: that no company can guarantee a worker a job for life; that the most important asset for both the worker and for the company is knowledge; and that, as technology and working methods change ever more swiftly, a worker continually needs to learn new skills.

The Economist estimated that United States spending on corporate education was growing at 5 per cent a year and that companies were spending $50 billion a year on education and training—about half the total United States higher education spending.

The management consultancy Arthur D. Little now offers a masters degree in management. A Quality Dynamics survey of 100 companies found that a third were planning to start granting degrees. Motorola has worked with Northwestern University's Kellogg School of Business to create a special manufacturing course. Nynex, the New York telecommunications company, has designed a telecommunications degree in conjunction with the State University of New York. And a group of companies is now offering satellite postgraduate education through a company—the National Technological University.

In fact, the notion of learning on the job is hardly new. IBM's corporate motto, when it set out to be the world's first genuine learning company, was 'Think'. The legendary GM boss Alfred Sloan appointed managers to disseminate learning around the organisation, as did ICI and other major British and Australian companies.

But the sea change occurring at present goes much further than just improving the way in which workers are trained. The change affects how we communicate within companies, how workers are treated and how management authority is derived.

First, communication. A learning organisation must be an organisation with open and thorough communication. Vertical and horizontal barriers to communication must be removed for a learning organisation to harness its capacities. Workers on the shopfloor need to be able to take suggestions about how things can be improved to the top and know that they will be listened to.

Some years ago I was working with a very large manufacturing company which was having quality problems with its exports to China. The managers had held several meetings and had discussed quality circles and various other measures to rectify the situation. One manager even thought the problem might be with the customers and not the company. The machine producing the products was old and a significant capital investment could have transformed its capacity, but it was still—except for the quality problem—paying its way. I suggested to the plant manager that we ought to go down to the machine and have a look at it. When we got there he struck up a conversation with one of the employees operating the machine. The employee was a longserving staff member who had worked on the machine for some years. When told about the problem he laconically replied that he was not really surprised.

He thought the problem stemmed from the fact that, some years before, one of the managers had ordered the machine setup to be changed so that the end product was packed in a slightly different—and inferior—way. 'Now, if you did it this way . . .', he said, and proceeded to demonstrate. The problem was solved. A vertical communication barrier had been removed.

Horizontal communication barriers are just as important. With the delayering of management many people have few peers to talk with. Finding ways for them to communicate across business units, and ways for them to share knowledge and experience, increases their effectiveness and eliminates some of the loneliness and isolation of the surviving middle managers in delayered organisations.

Second, learning organisations have to be sincere about believing in the dignity of work and the dignity of workers. You can't ask people to learn and to act intelligently, but treat them like automata.

Third, managers in a learning organisation cannot derive their authority solely from their position and power. They must derive it from their knowledge and their willingness to learn from others. As Peter Roberts said in the September *Australian Financial Review* article: 'This is where we get back to the traditional manager sitting in splendid isolation in an enclosed office and protected from prying eyes by secretaries and assistants. Such an executive is probably learning more slowly than those staff in the flexible work teams they oversee'.

Many management writers have grappled with how to define the learning organisation. In the *Harvard Business Review* of July–August 1993, David A. Garvin of the Harvard Business School reviewed the literature on building learning organisations. He found dozens of definitions, lots of books and little agreement.

He came to two important conclusions. First, that 'learning organisations cultivate the art of open, attentive listening and that managers must be open to criticism'. Second, that 'learning organisations are skilled at five main activities: systematic problem solving, experimenting with new approaches, learning from their own experience and past history, learning from the experience and best practices of others, and transferring knowledge quickly and efficiently through the organisation'.

Companies and organisations with these characteristics are light years away from the traditional hierarchical structures of the past. They are also light years away from many of today's companies—those which still espouse a cult of management that invests managers with all the wisdom, knowledge and leadership needed to make things happen. In the 21st century the most successful companies are probably going to be those in which a shopfloor worker or frontdesk person can tell the CEO, 'You're wrong, and this is why', and know that they will not only keep their job but also achieve change.

Off with his head!—the end of the dictatorial leader

Once we prize values and diversity, learn humility in planning and create a learning culture, we can do something about one of the biggest barriers to change in many organisations—re-educating the CEO.

The basic problem with most top managers is the very old-fashioned word for describing them: 'boss'. The boss is someone who drives people, directs them, says 'I' a lot, knows how things are done, gives orders and often takes the credit—in terms of salary packages and share participation schemes—for success. In the 21st century, successful companies won't need bosses. They'll need leaders.

Telstra, Australia's largest telecommunications company, has taken this to its logical extension by setting up a Centre for Leadership and a series of leadership programs. Dr Debby King, head of the Centre, says: 'A leader is not necessarily a person with all the answers but someone who can listen well and work with people'. Each year Telstra goes out to universities and colleges around Australia to identify the leaders of tomorrow and then offer them scholarships and work. Telstra doesn't choose these people just on the basis of academic success. It uses a sophisticated approach which allows it to gauge the personality of the candidates. The successful candidates are the candidates who best demonstrate the capacity to embrace the new concept of leadership—of achieving goals by working with people rather than by just directing them.

The Australian Government commissioned a major report on Australian management from a group headed by a CRA executive, David Karpin.[36] This group, too, focused on the approach to leadership which emphasises teamwork and co-operation rather than direction.

The new approach is a refreshing change in a country that had earlier been afflicted by considerable labour unrest—largely derived from the imported attitudes of United Kingdom managements and unions. Before the Great Strike of 1926 in the United Kingdom, Winston Churchill quipped that he had never met men so stupid and shortsighted as the mining union leaders—until he met the mine owners. Much later, in the 1960s, Harold Wilson said that the problems at British Leyland were created by management and unions—only to find the quote used again and again, in sections of the media, with the word 'management' left out!

The reality is that, under the old approach, management could blame workers or unions for its failures. With the new leadership paradigm it cannot escape so readily.

In the *Australian Financial Review* of 13 September 1995 Professor Bill Ford of the University of New South Wales said: 'Management's role is to set the overall strategy for the enterprise and to support rather than direct the front-line troops who impact on customers'. Ford pointed out that one of the manifestations of this approach is the increasing number of companies with open-plan offices. Hewlett-Packard has open-plan layouts with managers sitting at desks little different from those of everyone else in the company. The world's most successful private company—the Mars petfood and confectionery business—has open-plan offices for all its staff. Optus, the new telecommunications entrant into the Australian market, also uses an office layout designed to break down barriers and speed communications.

Christopher Bartlett, a professor at Harvard Business School, and Sumanthra Ghoshal, a professor at London Business School, wrote in the May–June 1995 issue of *Harvard Business Review* that 'the most basic task of corporate leaders is to unleash the human spirit which makes initiative, creativity and entrepreneurship possible'.

In their article they compared two companies: Norton, an industrial abrasives company, and its competitor 3M. Norton was a company that adopted a series of the latest management techniques and systems but whose diversification efforts never met expectations. In 1990 it was taken over by a French company, Compagnie de Saint-Gobian. 3M, by the mid-1980s, had sales eight times those of Norton. While in recent years 3M itself has faced problems, it has continued to focus on innovation and entrepreneurship.

The comparison indicated that Norton was 'an archetype of a systems-driven company, 3M epitomised a people-centred entrepreneurial model'. The authors concluded that 3M's top management saw its role as less one of directing and controlling employees' activities and more one of developing their initiatives and supporting their ideas. In other words, it saw its role as coach and nurturer rather than as boss.

The outcome was more than just increased sales—it was also a culture which managed to create a series of new products and services, year in and year out, to meet new customer needs. 3M's success with new products was in part a function of understanding customers, but it was primarily a result of the company creating an environment in which creativity and innovation were encouraged and rewarded. Today every one of us flags that success when we post those little yellow stickers on memos, books and articles in magazines.

A similar approach was outlined in the *Harvard Business Review* (September–October 1989) when Jack Welch, CEO of General Electric, said: 'Above all else . . . good leaders are open. They go up, down and around their organisations to reach people. It is all about human beings coming to see and accept things through a constant interactive process aimed at consensus'.

We saw earlier that one of the chief characteristics of the coming age is the real threat posed by fear, anxiety and a sense of alienation. In traditional organisations this alienation is compounded by people's authority and accountability being circumscribed and their status and dignity reduced to that of someone who just takes orders. People respond to such anxiety and alienation by searching for a place to belong, a place to be secure and a place in which they are respected. In the 21st century the successful company will be one that provides a sense of belonging.

The first step in doing this is for the CEO to get out of his or her office and demonstrate that he or she cares about people, respects them and listens to them. The second step occurs when the CEO rejects the language of 'the boss'. Instead of giving directions and orders the CEO starts to be a leader who coaches, uses goodwill and enthusiasm to motivate people, talks about 'we' instead of 'I', develops people rather than uses them, and makes time for the things that count—the people in the company. Success in this new approach comes when the CEO demonstrates the reality of the approach by matching the language with his or her deeds—when the CEO becomes a leader who creates cultures rather than dictating policies.

The new leader is a culture creator, not a policy dictator

If the leader is not to be just a boss who gives orders but rather someone who encourages successful business outcomes then the most important task facing the leader is culture creation. Such a culture cannot be created by promulgation—by simply stating a policy as to what the culture will be—because that is a negation of everything the successful culture should comprise. But establishing the right culture does require some definition of what it is and how it might look. The first difficulty in this is to define what the term 'culture' itself means. Today we use the concept in a host of different ways.

Its origins really lie with the early sociologists such as Max

Weber. Weber's most important book was *The Protestant Ethic and the Spirit of Capitalism*,[37] and in it he showed how a particular culture—Protestantism—encouraged the creation of a particular economic system. In effect, he argued that intellectual ideas create values and cultures which shape behaviour, and that this then shapes the social system in which we live. In this sense the sociological theory of culture is about developing a bridge between ideas and values and the structure of society.

Today that is exactly what culture creation within companies and organisations is all about: having the intellectual ideas which shape values and attitudes; using those values and attitudes to shape behaviour; and then having that behaviour produce the desired outcomes.

How can leaders put the theory into practice?

First, by their own approach to communication. Leaders who are seen to be listening, and seen to be practising two-way communication, are demonstrating that the corporate culture is open and responsive.

Second, by demonstrating that everyone can learn. CEOs need to be among the people who go on courses—just like everybody else—to enhance their knowledge. A CEO needs to be seen to be learning from other people in the organisation. It is, for instance, highly probable that, if a company needs to know something about what is fashionable among the young, then younger staff members are more likely to be able to provide that expertise than the average CEO is. The CEO should be the first to ask the office juniors about the latest trends.

Third, by connecting with the reality of the daily lives of customers and staff. One of the most devastating blows to the world's most powerful CEO, President George Bush, came during a Presidential election campaign when he visited a supermarket. He was entranced by the bar-code reading capacity of the checkout machines and enthused about how this new technology showed United States leadership and innovation. As he enthused it became obvious that the President had not been in a supermarket for a very long time! He demonstrated that—in one of the most basic areas of human experience today—he no longer had experience. In effect, he proclaimed to the voters: 'I am out of touch with ordinary life'. In contrast, Percy Barnevik, the CEO of one of the world's most successful multinationals, ABB, says he spends up to 60 per cent of his time out of his office talking with the company's staff, and aims to talk personally to about 6500 people a year.

Fourth, by understanding and defining what the CEO can and should do. A New Jersey management consulting firm, Kepner-Tregoe, recently undertook a major survey of views of how successful change was from the perspective of both top management and staff. The study revealed that to encourage the sorts of behaviour which most enhance a culture a CEO should:

- evolve, articulate and commit to a common set of values
- provide a strategic context
- establish a special contract between the organisation and its employees, in which mutuality is the key and in which both sides have responsibilities
- design the right performance environment so that the right behaviours are rewarded and the rewards are seen to be fair and just
- build an infrastructure which supports knowledge and information sharing
- create a learning organisation

In such an environment the leader needs to learn some old-fashioned humility. The arrogance which can come from command is simply not conducive to a learning culture. CEOs who can say, 'I was wrong', or who can demonstrate that they want to learn from the most junior of the increasingly diverse range of people in their companies or from the smallest of their culturally diverse range of customers . . . these are CEOs well on the way to moving from policy dictation to culture creation.

A company's vision and values are what encapsulate and act as a consistent reference post for the culture created.

Using vision and values to deliver corporate focus

Sir Isaiah Berlin is a distinguished philosopher and historian of ideas. Over the years he has been one of the most prominent academic voices arguing that there are alternatives to the post-Enlightenment view of the world—a view that shapes so much political and economic thought. He has excavated the ideas of thinkers to whom nation and community, and religious values, have been important, and he has pointed out their relevance to a society facing the uncertainty of the new millennium.

One of the things that has driven much of Berlin's research is the comment of the Greek poet, Archilochus, that 'the fox knows many things but the hedgehog knows one big thing'. Berlin interprets the comment as conveying the importance of a universal explanation—a central organising vision. Unlike the hedgehog the fox pursues many trails, 'seizing upon the essence of a vast variety of experiences and objects for what they are in themselves', without trying to fit them to a vision.

Today many companies face a similar problem—a problem they need to overcome if they are to be focused on how to succeed in the post-Enlightenment environment that the 21st century is set to create. That problem is how to ensure that a company protects its values and how it can achieve a central corporate focus.

Peter Wildblood, author of *Leading From Within*,[38] has done much to help companies build a sense of purpose among all staff. He writes:

> Real 'control' of performance is based on a well understood sense of purpose by all the staff about the overall direction of the team or organisation. When this is combined with a

> clearly defined set of operating principles, control can occur without a lot of direct management intervention.

This is the fundamental rationale for developing a coherent and effective vision and set of values—to ensure that, like the hedgehog, there is 'one big thing' that the whole company knows. Admittedly, cynicism about vision and values is often found at every level of a company. But the evidence seems overwhelming that a clearly articulated statement of them does provide the core focus a company needs.

Harvard Business School's John Kotter has written several books about corporate culture and performance and has travelled the world talking about how companies can transform themselves. One of the most succinct statements of his views appeared in the *Harvard Business Review* article, 'Why Transformation Efforts Fail' (March–April 1995). Kotter says the conclusions he draws about transformation are based on the study of more than 100 companies which have tried to make themselves into better competitors. He lists ten barriers to transformation and eight steps needed to transform an organisation. In both lists he focuses on vision. He says:

> In every successful transformation effort that I have seen, the guiding coalition develops a picture of the future that is relatively easy to communicate and appeals to customers, stockholders and employees. In failed transformations you often find plenty of plans and directives and programs but no vision.

A Stanford University academic, James Collins, surveyed 700 CEOs to find out which companies they had learned from. All the companies specified had strong corporate cultures, were rarely led by charismatic leaders and were driven to make an impact on society, not just make a profit. In a recent book,[39] *Built to Last: Successful Habits of Visionary Companies,* he explodes myths about vision and performance. Overwhelmingly he finds that vision is not the product of extraordinary insight on the part of some visionary leader—rather it is a product of the development of core values which all members of the organisation agree with and adhere to.

How can you create such a vision? Often the vision and values statement will start as a very rough draft prepared by one individual. Often it will be evolved from detailed research and extensive consultation. Very rarely, it can be summed up in one word like IBM's original 'Think'. Too often, however, the recipe for creating a vision is like the advice, given by a very old gardener at a large English country house, on how to create the perfect lawn. It was really quite simple, he said. Just cultivate the soil, put in some fertiliser, plant the seed, and then mow it and roll it . . . for a few hundred years. Often a vision statement is written by someone glib with words but not necessarily familiar with the company—which explains why many statements sound like identikit combinations of pat phrases about customer focus and added value.

There are two approaches that can help you to formulate the right words for a vision. Both involve getting together a cross-section of the staff. The first approach is to ask them to think of words which describe the company now and as they would like to see it in the future. Then you just write down the words and talk until you get consensus about the key ones. Then it is a matter of translating those words into phrases. Often you find the phrases from this process provide the foundation for an effective vision. The second approach locks more into people's imagination. In this case you ask the team to think of world-famous people who epitomise the character of the company now and as they would like to see it in the future. (You can use animals instead of famous people.) Again you generate a list but this time you derive the words by asking the team what the names mean in terms of words. From there it is again a process of words to phrases to vision.

It is now vitally important to thoroughly research the vision statement among target audiences to ensure that it makes sense. We are all familiar with the experience of a group who go away on a creative workshop and—through the effects of bonding and isolation—come up with what seems like a brilliant idea. On returning to the real world everybody wonders what on earth they had been taking when they created it! Research is the vision reality check.

A vision is a powerful tool. Its effectiveness is demonstrated in how we live our daily lives. Day in and day out we act by a moral code. We don't need laws and regulations to encourage us to act in particular ways because we have internalised the code. And that's the secret of a successful vision. We must first identify the internalised code that guides the behaviour of a company and then put it into the words that describe what the company wants to be. The next step is to ensure that the company's structure matches the vision—that the chorus is singing about what's actually happening on stage.

That involves not only the company's own structure but also the structure of its relationships with other companies.

Duck! The organisational pendulum is swinging back

In a chaotic and uncertain business environment one thing is certain—there is a lot that can go wrong. Rapid changes in a market, crises, dishonesty, incompetence and stupidity can all contribute to massive losses in organisations. This has been true of business for as long as it has operated, but the scale of business today makes the scale of the disaster that much more significant.

One of Britain's oldest banks—Baring Brothers—was destroyed by the actions of a rogue trader, Nick Leeson, in Singapore and the lack of controls in the bank. In Australia an old-established company, AWA, suffered massive foreign exchange losses. In France a government-owned company, Credit Lyonnaise, was crippled by investments in Hollywood. In Germany a highly successful metals company, Metallgesellschaft, lost billions through commodity speculation in the United States. The film business has often been a disaster, of course, and the stately Deutsche Bank had a costly involvement in film as far back as the making of Fritz Lang's *Metropolis.*

The vast majority of crises confronting companies are no longer caused by technological failure or natural disasters but through human error.

The Institute for Crisis Management in Louisville, Kentucky, undertook an analysis of 31 500 United States business stories appearing in the media in 1989 and 1990, compared with a decade before. The analysis showed that most of the crises were due to 'mismanagement' rather than 'operational' crises. In the 10 years there was a 196 per cent increase in bad press for business due to consumer activism, a 122 per cent increase due to whistleblowing and a 125 per cent increase in stories based on court decisions.

Our standards of engineering excellence may be outstanding, but people still make errors.

In a millenarian age when extremes become commonplace the risks facing companies are enormous. Most company structures are not designed to cope with such stresses and uncertainties—they are products of history and organisational fads more than of purposeful design.

In the 1960s and 1970s the fashion was for conglomerates. The business press adulated the managers, such as Harold Geneen, who built massive companies straddling disparate industries in different nations. These managers were believed to be able, simply by management ability, to transform companies and achieve more from them. There are still some such companies—notably the United Kingdom's Hanson Group, although even this is now being split up following the death of one of the founders.

By the 1980s conglomerates had become unfashionable. Partly in the search for profits from financial manoeuvring, many were taken over, broken up and sold off. Where conglomerates stayed together their various business units were given more and more autonomy, and this was pushed further and further down the line.

In the late 1980s and early 1990s 'focus' became the key structural motivator. Influenced by Professor Michael Porter's extensive work on competitive advantage and core competences, companies started to ask what their core businesses were and what they no longer needed. The non-core assets were sold off and non-core services contracted out.

Porter made famous the story of the Pullman Car company which manufactured the luxury railroad cars that went across the United States midwest (and featured in so many films). The Pullman company failed because it thought it was in the *rail carriage* business and not in the *transportation* business. Equally, the 19th century gaslight companies that thought they were in the *gas* business failed in the face of competition from new electricity companies which knew they were in the *lighting and power* industry.

But, as is implicit in these two examples, core competence can act as a link for many different activities. The Kodak company's core competence is imaging; the range of consumer, commercial and technical products it provides under this umbrella is huge, even after its recent successful divestments.

Most major companies still cover a wide range of activities, goods and services. BHP—Australia's biggest company—is a resource company whose resource focus has led it into mining, energy, technology and metal manufacturing. Computer companies such as Hewlett-Packard have been a success by focusing on their quality printers but have also diversified into computer software and hardware and computer support.

Because no one individual can manage such disparate businesses, devolution has been essential and most successful companies operate on the basis of a small head office and separate business units.

Today, however, the pendulum is beginning to swing back from the high degree of autonomy towards a more centralised approach in which the head office acts as the linchpin of a network of linked operations.

The reasons are obvious. First, mistakes are more common in chaotic environments in which people have more freedom. And mistakes in large companies today can be massive.

The second reason is a technological one. With modern accounting and communication systems it is possible to centralise control much more effectively. Managers in business units may well have considerable autonomy in decision-making, but the capacity to instantaneously know the financial implications of decisions is one that no sensible company would fail to acquire. Using internal market systems in which bids for resources are constantly tested is another way of combining centralisation with devolved autonomy. And new thinking is allowing companies to focus on the real questions about head offices—questions about how much value they add and what they do, rather than how big they are.

Third, companies increasingly need to operate with community consent—with the approval of the community. To achieve this, management must ensure that brand values and corporate image are rigorously and consistently maintained. Some form of centralised control—cultural, financial or whatever—becomes essential to this process.

Finally, economies of scale still exist and many companies are finding that real cost savings can be achieved by taking support functions back into corporate centres and eliminating their duplication in business units.

The capacity to plan and control for the future may be limited by chaos. Yet the demands for closer supervision are increased by the uncertainties of the new millennium. The keys to resolving the dilemma are technological and cultural. Companies must use modern communications to work more closely with devolved units. They must also maintain a culture that unifies the company around core values while fostering productive diversity.

The best way of seeing how this can be achieved is by examining the best features of small business and observing how successful companies can get bigger while still thinking like a small business.

Small businesses proliferate. They open and close and they cause huge headaches for proprietors, bankers and governments. While regarded by many as a good thing, unfortunately they often fail because of lack of finance or lack of experience.

Successful small businesses, however, are very interesting organisations which have features of great significance to big business. First, they focus on the basics. These can range from a set of basic skills and products through to the most basic and essential financial control tools. Second, they must generate cash regularly and in sufficient quantities to avoid the need to call on unsympathetic banks and financiers. Third, they concentrate on what they are best at, rather than pursuing a host of diverse and unconnected activities. Fourth, they keep lines of communication short and ensure that the managers are an integral part of the total company team rather than a separate part. Fifth, they tend to have a strong common culture forged by the founder or the owners.

These five characteristics—focusing on the basics (including financial control), cash generation, concentrating on what you do best, good communication and teamwork, and a strong organisational culture—are the characteristics of a business able to resolve the dilemma of being flexible, devolving authority and still maintaining the centralised control necessary to avoid the unexpected disaster.

Co-operation and competition—partnerships and performance

The doyen of management writers, Peter Drucker, once said that 'adversarial power relationships work only if you never have to see or work with the bastards again'.

In today's business environment it is unusual for anyone to have that luxury. Companies strive to achieve repeat business from customers in order to maximise profitability and minimise marketing expenditure. Contractor and supplier arrangements are designed to bring company and supplier closer together in order to permit the use of just-in-time manufacturing schedules and to meet quality standards. In some industries—especially telecommunications and computing—a competitor in one market is an ally or a supplier in another.

Over the years, of course, many companies have aspired

to various forms of collaboration with competitors. Unfortunately, the aspiration is sometimes converted into actual collusion. Adam Smith remarked in *The Wealth of Nations* that 'people of the same trade seldom meet together, even for merriment and diversion, [without] the conversation [ending] in a conspiracy against the public, or in some contrivance to raise prices'. Today anti-competition law and higher standards of ethical behaviour mean that the vast majority of companies avoid such collusion.

The sort of constructive co-operation outside the company that we are talking about is really an extension of the concepts of learning, teamwork and partnership within companies. Typical examples of such successful partnerships and alliances today are found in the defence, airline and automotive industries, among others.

The United States deficit and the end of the Cold War mean that defence companies can no longer survive on the basis of selling thousand-dollar hammers to the Air Force or in the light of massive cost overruns. They are now being exposed to the competition and demands for efficiency that the rest of us face. To some extent they are achieving this by merger, but they are also resorting to strategic alliances in which partners blend their expertise. A proposed agreement between Aerospatiale and Daimler-Benz Aerospace on missiles and satellites is a good example of this.

In the airline business, continuing national regulations sometimes limit the opportunities for merger. The alternative approach here has been to *begin* with a merger—as British Airways did—and then follow with alliances and strategic shareholdings, as BA has with the Australian airline Qantas.

In the automotive industry, the strategic alliances are best illustrated by the bewildering range of rebadging arrangements that apply. Are you driving a Ford or a Mazda, and did the key components come from a common roster of suppliers?

Some countries have virtually built their economies on strategic alliances. The Japanese *keiretsu* system and the interlocking shareholdings between German companies are forms of alliance. United States companies are now following suit. The management consultancy Booz Allen and Hamilton has estimated that in the five years from 1987 to 1992 the number of formal alliances in America increased from less than a thousand to some 20 000. In an uncertain environment the risks of competition can be immense. The effectively wasted investment in competing video cassette formats and then in high definition television indicates how billions can be invested and then lost. In Australia two companies are installing optical fibre cable to provide pay television and other services in a nation with a population of 18 million—probably barely enough to support one network provider.

Provided that the consumer is not defrauded by collusive behaviour, co-operation can make more sense to countries, companies and the consumers than mindless competition. Most importantly co-operation encourages companies to focus on what they do best rather than what they would like to do—or what makes their managers think they are the biggest and toughest players in the jungle.

So, how can we make co-operation work?

First, by basing the co-operation on a virtue of key importance in a millenarian age—trust. One of the features of an age of uncertainty and change is fear. In the corporate environment the fear can be of losing a contract, of losing face or of being taken advantage of. No partnership or alliance can survive without trust. Trust can't be created by developing huge contracts specifying every last detail of an arrangement. But it can be built on the basis of openness, listening, friendship and a commitment to co-operation.

Second, by ensuring that our communications work. By keeping partners informed, the chance of surprises—which unsettle relationships—is limited.

Third, by taking a long-term view. Building trust takes time. When parties seek short-term advantage the capacity to build long-term relationships is reduced.

Fourth, by being respectful of diverse cultures. Most alliances require that not only different companies work together but also different people, different cultures and different nationalities. Unless we understand—and respect—the differences, trust becomes impossible.

Finally, the real barrier to co-operation is the 'zero-sum game' mentality we noted earlier—the desire to kill, crush or conquer the competitor. Once we rid our language and our thinking of military metaphors we are on the way to creating an environment in which trust and co-operation can flourish.

And as we learn to co-operate with partners outside the business we also need to learn how to co-operate with business' most important partners—the people within the company.

How to stop treating Generation MM as just another cost

In the 1970s and 1980s an Australian company demonstrated that treating people as more than just another cost can pay off. And it did so in the midst of turbulent conditions affecting both its neighbours and its major competitors. The company was Amcor Limited and its success was achieved at its Maryvale pulp and paper mill—the biggest in Australia—in the Latrobe Valley in Victoria.

The Latrobe Valley is an industrial area dominated by male blue collar workers. It has strong unions with a history of militancy. For decades the area's biggest employer was the State-owned electricity commission, the SECV (now being privatised). The Amcor mill was the biggest private sector employer. At almost exactly the same time, the SECV and Amcor decided to expand their respective plants. In the case of the SECV the plan was to build a new power generation station at Loy Yang. Amcor planned to build a world-scale pulp mill.

The Amcor mill was built on time and on budget and was officially opened by the State Premier of the day. The SECV plant became the centre of one of the State's longest and most vicious industrial disputes, culminating in a lockout which cost the State of Victoria and the workers millions and millions of dollars.

The geographic area was the same, the workers in the mill and in the electricity industry were neighbours and shared similar backgrounds, and many of the trade unions in the Valley were represented on both sites. Yet the outcomes were radically different.

That this was not just some Latrobe Valley phenomenon is shown by another comparison. In the 1980s Amcor's major competitor—Australian Pulp and Paper Mills (APPM)—set out to change the work practices at its Burnie mill in Tasmania. The changes it wanted had already been introduced at Amcor's Maryvale mill without a day lost in industrial action. This was despite the fact that the changes had resulted in both employee redundancies and alterations in long-maintained conditions and privileges. At Burnie the same attempt to bring about change resulted in a major strike, riots outside the mill, and the very rare sight of a conservative State Premier supporting the picketing workers against the company. Once again the outcomes were radically different.

Understanding the difference allows us to grasp some important lessons for companies in the 21st century.

First, both SECV and APPM managers were driven partly by ideology. They believed the rhetoric about the right of management to manage and the need to bring about far-reaching change in order to make Australia more competitive. They preached the lessons of the new band of right-wing political leaders who were determined to transform Australian society. And they believed that changing the workers was the way to achieve a more competitive future. Implicit in the ideology was that past problems were the workers' fault. Amcor, on the other hand, had a far more pragmatic approach. It wanted change because it wanted to build a better business. It explained the benefits of the better business to the employees and worked with them to bring about change.

Second, the SECV and APPM spent a lot more time talking to government, the media and the wider community than they did to their own employees. In the case of APPM, a team of senior managers jetted around the tiny Tasmanian State in the corporate jet, holding media conferences and telling the world what they were up to. Amcor rarely talked to the outside world at all, and the first that people—other than its employees—knew about the change was when the Burnie situation erupted. An enterprising young journalist decided that it might be a good idea to find out what Australia's other paper company was doing about the need for change and whether it anticipated any problems. The journalist was surprised to discover that the change had already occurred.

Third, Amcor had started the change process at Maryvale by focusing on the customer. The company spent almost a year on this exercise, which made it easier to communicate to staff the need for change in all areas of operation.

And, finally, Amcor had a strong and proud culture. Managers and staff were proud of being part of the company and the culture encouraged trust, loyalty and a sense of dignity among employees.

Unfortunately, around the world the Amcor example has been the exception.

Writing in the *London Review of Books* of 2 November 1995, the economic historian Edward Luttwak highlighted two realities in American manufacturing. He pointed out that on 10 August 1995 Boeing had its shares quoted on the New York Stock Exchange at $65. This was 77 times earnings. The shares of its nearest aerospace competitor, McDonnel Douglas, were selling at 15 times earnings. On the same day the PE ratio for General Electric was just 19. But in the very same week, Luttwak noted, the International Association of Machinists and Aerospace Workers—a union which represents 34 650 Boeing employees—had surveyed its members. The survey found that just over 20 per cent of the workforce thought their jobs were 'somewhat secure' and that more than 50 per cent thought their jobs were 'not secure'.

The Economist reported on 6 January 1996 that a United States consultancy, Challenger Gray and Christmas, had calculated that the United States had seen three million retrenchments between the late 1980s and 1995. In the same week AT&T announced that it had plans to lay off 40 000 people including 24 000 managers. Significantly, the same consultants were reported, in *The Economist* of 20 April 1996, as having found that all the downsizing had in fact had relatively little impact on profitability and productivity. Fewer than half of the companies which downsized after 1990 went on to report higher profits and even fewer saw higher productivity.

In contrast, a Massachusetts consultant, Montor, found that nine out of ten firms which outperformed their industries over a decade had experienced no more than one reorganisation and no change in CEO.

The reasons—in retrospect—are obvious. Destroying jobs also destroys loyalty and deprives companies of invaluable corporate memory—memory about processes, products, people and markets—on which profit is often heavily based.

This destruction of people's jobs came despite the fact that in the past decade or so businesses spent an enormous amount of time allegedly communicating with staff. For much of the 1980s businesses talked about issues such as quality and empowerment. It became fashionable to regard staff—along with investors, communities and governments—as stakeholders. As stakeholders, it was recognised, they had an interest in the company, and management needed to take serious note of that interest.

And then came the recession.

Under schemes bearing a variety of names, staff were laid off. In some cases it was called downsizing, in others it was re-engineering, in others again it was called rightsizing. But, whatever it was called, staff lost their jobs and companies demonstrated that—when it came to the bottom line—staff weren't stakeholders but were just another cost.

The result of this has been, understandably, that many remaining staff have adverse attitudes towards their employers. Many of them suffer from a survivor mentality; many of them are alienated and many of them are distrustful.

United States surveys described in *PR Reporter* during 1995 indicate the dimensions of the problem. Over the past 20 years there has been a drop of 20 percentage points—from 47 per cent to 27 per cent—in the number of employees who say they are extremely satisfied with the work they chose to do. Some 45 per cent of employees feel that 'the interests of employees and employers are by their very nature opposed'. Eighty per cent of employees say they feel some personal loyalty to their employer but only 37 per cent consider the loyalty to be reciprocated. Some 28 per cent do not look forward to their work week. Sixty per cent of people in their thirties want to turn back the clock and change their careers.

Another employee survey, of 200 communication specialists, found that the most common call was for management to rebuild a sense of trust.

And in one of its studies the management consulting firm Kepner-Tregoe found that management was deluding itself if it thought that staff reacted well to change and to new business initiatives. The survey found that in the previous five years 89 per cent of organisations had experienced six or more initiatives designed to improve organisational efficiency. The perceptions of these initiatives by top management groups and by employees were quite different, as the figures given in the table show.

INITIATIVE DID NOT MEET EXPECTATIONS

	Executives %	Workers %
Empowerment/involvement	5	21
Culture change	8	25
Performance systems change	9	27
Developing skills/competencies	4	13
Productivity improvement	5	13
Restructuring	4	20
Downsizing/cost reduction	8	16
Total quality	6	16

POSITIVE EFFECT OF INITIATIVE

	Executives %	Workers %
Profitability	67	43
Quality	64	44
Customer satisfaction	60	40
Competitiveness	60	36
Internal systems	33	22
Organisational structure	52	27
Workforce skills	44	24

The lesson to be drawn from the figures is obvious—much of the workforce regards employers' actions with a great deal of cynicism and a lack of trust. Rebuilding that trust is going to be a big task in the 21st century. The starting point will need to be the rekindling of loyalty—loyalty to employees and then loyalty to companies. Companies may have to rediscover their soul and start putting human values on the same level as financial values.

We have already seen that the successful 21st century company will be a learning organisation which demonstrates that it is flexible and able to harness the abilities of people. It will need to be able to demonstrate that it cares about people and demonstrate that it is committed to two-way communication with staff.

The goal can't be achieved by trying to re-establish lifelong employment—a goal which many staff themselves would not favour. However, a recent business roundtable, organised by the US Work/Family Directions organisation and involving Boston-based companies, provided some hints as to how it might be achieved.

First, a company can provide benefits that address important personal and family needs—not in a paternalistic way, but in a way that helps people to get the balance in their life right.

Second, it can encourage greater flexibility in the workplace. It is no good saying to people: we can no longer offer you lifetime employment, steady career advancement and increasing salaries—instead we want you to work harder and smarter, be ready to change whenever we say, and provide better customer service. If the company wants flexibility from its staff it must provide flexibility in return.

Third, it must build commitment to teamwork. It is unlikely that complete loyalty to the company can be recreated overnight, or at all. Most people in any case tend to be more highly committed to the team they work with, and the job itself, than they are to their employer.

Finally, we need to reward people for accepting change. Senior managers receive massive pay and share option packages for slashing jobs and costs. America has created a very rich one per cent of the population while at the same time seven out of ten Americans have seen their real hourly pay decline, with a substantial minority—12 per cent—remaining in poverty even though fully employed. The people who suffer the changes and the job losses are also entitled to incentives for performing in the new ways that are considered necessary.

The alternative is to reignite the class war between employer and employee—first at the company level, then at the industry level and finally at the national level. The surveys indicate that many of today's workers are becoming susceptible again to the logic and language of class war.

And it would be ironic indeed if the system that had supposedly triumphed in the Cold War, towards the end of the 20th century, was the system that precipitated a massive Generation MM worker backlash against itself in the 21st.

Postscript: The hangover after the millennium

In the next few years, as the millennium gets closer, expectations about it will grow, diversify and multiply. Sects that we have not yet heard of will convince millions that some disaster is just around the corner and will put forward simple—but mystical—solutions. Myths will abound as to what the year 2000 will hold. The story, recounted earlier, about computers and their alleged inability to turn over from 1999 to 2000 will lead to predictions of collapsing systems and global chaos. Every special interest group will argue that the year 2000 ought to be marked in some way special to *them.*

There is of course a possibility that something totally unforeseen might happen on 31 December 1999. The millenarians might be right! It could be a meteorite crashing to earth from outer space, an outbreak of nuclear war started by some terrorist who has built a briefcase-size atomic bomb, a massive tidal wave wiping out Los Angles and Tokyo . . . or it could be something miraculous that simply never occurred to us.

But most probably life—as people accepted before Zoroaster made humans first think about millenarianism—will seem to just go on. The world will wake up on 1 January 2000 with nothing but a giant hangover to show for it all. When that happens we will have another problem—the anticlimax of unfulfilled expectations.

But we should not assume that this anticlimax will be the end of it all. Those predicting the transformation of the world are rarely discouraged by unfulfilled prophecies. Indeed, sometimes the lack of fulfilment makes them even more convinced in their belief than they were before.

So it will be with the world and the new millennium. By 31 December 1999 everyone will know—and feel—that the coming year is different. Whether the morning after is an anticlimax or not, they'll get up and set out into the new century with the confidence that every new generation has in its capacity to remake the world.

This book has sought to tell you how you can be ready for that moment when Generation MM sets out to remake the world.

It will be a world characterised by a mixture of amazing technology and mysticism; a world characterised by a search for values and a demand that organisations demonstrate that values have an integral part in everything they do.

But it will also be a world of opportunity—a world in which intelligent organisations and intelligent people can prosper as never before. Instead of scoffing at the sight of church leaders and environmentalists sitting down to talk about the apocalypse, they will calmly think about what the new millennium means for their business. Instead of being disturbed and unsettled by diversity, they will embrace the changes as a means of boosting productivity and profitability and as a source of the sheer joy of a diverse and varied lifestyle. Instead of being frightened by change and uncertainty, they will recognise that understanding the limits of prediction and planning is not a weakness but a recognition of the kind of strength it takes to succeed in interesting times.

It will also be an opportunity not only to respond to the demands of Generation MM but also to prepare for the day when Generation MM provides the managers, the CEOs, the political leaders and the opinion leaders.

Being ready for all those opportunities is what will give you the Millennium Edge.

Notes

1 Malcolm Bull (ed.), *Acopalypse Theory and the End of the World* (Blackwell, 1995).
2 Norman Cohn, *The Pursuit of the Millennium* (Oxford University Press 1970).
3 Malcom Bull (ed.) op. cit.
4 G.W. Trompf (ed.), *Cargo Cults and Millenarian Movements* (Mouton de Gruyter, 1990).
5 Gore Vidal, *Armageddon?* (Andre Deutsch, 1987).
6 Christopher Hitchens, *Missionary Position* (Verso, 1995).
7 (Note 7 does not appear in the text.)
8 James Frazer, *Golden Bough* (Macmillan, 1890).
9 Eric Hobsbawm and Terence Ranger (eds), *The Invention of Tradition* (Cambridge University Press, 1983).
10 Natalie Zemon Davis, *Society and Culture in Early Modern France* (Stanford University Press, 1975).
11 Peter Burke, *The Fabrication of Louis XIV* (Yale University Press, 1992).
12 Lisa Jardine, *Erasmus Man of Letters* (Princeton University Press, 1993).
13 David Hackett Fisher, *Paul Revere's Ride* (Oxford University Press, 1994).
14 Paul Weaver, *News and Culture of Lying: How Journalism Really Works* (The Free Press, 1994).
15 John Stauber and Sheldon Rampton, *Toxic Sludge is Good for You* (Common Courage Press, 1995).
16 Susan B. Trento, *The Power House* (St Martin's Press, 1992).
17 Cynthia Crossen, *Tainted Truth: The Manipulation of Fact in America* (Simon & Schuster, 1994).

18 Mort Rosenblum, *Who Stole the News?* (John Wiley & Sons, 1993).
19 Marshall McLuhan, *The Global Village: Transformations in World Life and Media in the 21st Century* (Oxford University Press, NY, 1989).
20 Umberto Eco, *Foucault's Pendulum* (Secker & Warburg, 1989).
21 Ann Moyal, *Breakfast with Beaverbrook* (Melbourne University Press, 1994).
22 Simon Schama, *Landscape and Memory* (HarperCollins, 1995).
23 George Soros, *Soros on Soros* (John Wiley & Sons, 1995).
24 Michael Porter, *Competitive Strategy* (The Free Press, 1980); *Competitive Advantage* (The Free Press, 1985); *The Competitive Advantage of Nations* (Macmillan, 1990).
25 Amitaai Etzioni, *The Spirit of Community: Rights, Responsibility and the Communication Agenda* (Crown Publishers, 1993).
26 Warren Reed and Reg Little, *The Confucian Renaissance* (Federation Press, 1989).
27 James Womack, *The Machine that Changed the World: Based on the Massachusetts Institute of Technology 5-Million Dollar, 5-Year Study on the Future of the Automobile* (Rawson Associates, New York, 1990).
28 Sally Hegelsen, *The Female Advantage—Women's Ways of Readership* (Doubleday Currency, 1990).
29 Robert Neild, *The English, The French and the Oyster* (Quiller Press, 1995).
30 Adam Smith, *The Wealth of Nations* (Oxford University Press, 1976).
31 Joseph Badarracco Jnr., *Business Ethics: Roles and Responsibilities* (Richard Irwin, 1995).
32 Lois Hogan et al., *Rediscovering the Soul of Business: A Renaissance of Values* (New Readers Press, 1995).
33 Al Ries and Jack Trent, *Positioning: the Battle For Your Mind* (McGraw Hill, 1986).
34 Sun-Tsze, *The Art of War* (Oxford University Press, 1971).
35 Anthony Carnevale and Susan Stone, *American Mosaic: An Indepth Report on the Advantage of Diversity in the United States Workforce* (McGraw Hill, 1988).
36 David Karpin, *Enterprising Nation: Renewing Australia's Managers to Meet the Challenge of the Asia–Pacific Century* (Australian Government Publishing Service Canberra, 1995).
37 Max Weber, *The Protestant Ethic and the Spirit of Capitalism* (Allen & Unwin, 1976).
38 Peter Wildblood, *Leading from Within* (Allen & Unwin, 1994).
39 James Collins, *Built to Last: Successful Habits of Visionary Companies* (HarperCollins, 1994).